Enterprise Software TCO:
Calculating and Using Total Cost of Ownership for Decision Making

Shaun Snapp

For information about this title or to order other books and/or electronic media, contact the publisher:
SCM Focus Press
PO Box 29502 #9059
Las Vegas, NV 89126-9502
http://www.scmfocus.com/scmfocuspress
(408) 657-0249

ISBN: 978-1-939731-27-2

Printed in the United States of America

Cover and interior design by: 1106 Design

Contents

CHAPTER 1

Introduction

Let's make sure you bought the right book by getting an official definition as to what is total cost of ownership.

> *"Total cost of ownership (TCO) is a financial estimate*
> *intended to help buyers and owners determine the direct*

and indirect costs of a product or system. It is a management accounting concept that can be used in full cost accounting or even ecological economics where it includes social costs." — Wikipedia

The definition is, of course, the easy part; the more difficult part to explain to people is why TCO is so important. The reason for the necessity of TCO is that the "price tag" on an item does not tell you a lot about that item's long-term total cost. This is true generally, but enterprise software is the extreme example of this well-recognized purchasing reality. In fact, many different researchers have concluded that the software license cost will end up being less than 20% percent of the total amount the company will invest in the application (although the percentages vary quite a bit per software category and per individual software vendor).[1] In addition to the software license cost, there are implementation costs, support costs and maintenance costs. Without an understanding of TCO, there is a tendency to focus on acquisition costs—not only for enterprise software, but for any other item as well. George G. Stanley, the former USAF Principle Deputy for Logistics, highlighted this problem in a white paper in response to the US military having repeated problems with ERP implementation in multiple branches of service. In his paper, he noted the following about Department of Defense IT decision-making logic.

> *"Much of the attention paid to the DoD budgeting is focused on new systems acquisitions. But those of us with boots on the ground know that procurement accounts for only about $10 billion of the budget, while maintenance and operations comes to more than $60 billion."*

The idea for this book came about for three basic reasons. First, I could not find any books on the topic of enterprise software TCO. Second, in writing the book *Enterprise Software Selection: How to Pinpoint the Perfect Software Solution using Multiple Information Sources,* my personal experience was reinforced by broader research that shows most companies that implement enterprise software

---

[1] As software as a service (SaaS) becomes more prevalent, the cost of the software component will be increasingly difficult to track. This is because SaaS vendors do not sell a software license, but instead sell access to software and hardware. They may offer some complimentary consulting as well. This makes the total costs easier to track, but it makes the specific cost categories more difficult to track.

do not perform TCO analysis to support their software decision-making. In fact, quite the contrary; most implementing companies focus on the acquisition cost. Third, after researching material currently available in the field, I found the concept of TCO to have been manipulated by everyone from software vendors to IT analyst firms in order to meet their predetermined objectives—objectives that were promotional in nature.

It seems that many entities would prefer that companies not actually know their TCO, and instead present it as something dark and mysterious. Some of the criticisms that have been directed at TCO almost seem directed toward influencing companies away from calculating TCO because it's "hard." However, not only is it possible to calculate TCO; it is necessary and important to know TCO in order to make effective IT decisions. TCO is a durable concept, and the more you work with TCO, the more comfortable you will become with it.

This book is also connected to the SCM Focus Press book *Enterprise Software Risk: Controlling the Main Risk Factors on IT Projects,* as both this and software selection should leverage TCO estimation. At one point in this book we will discuss the importance of combining TCO estimations with risk estimation as well.

The interviews that I performed with people who have worked with the concept of TCO for more than a decade left me with the impression that they have become quite cynical about TCO, due to the easily traceable financial bias of the individuals and companies performing TCO analysis. Interestingly, much as within the financial industry, in information technology the entities that have made some of most gerrymandered TCO calculations are some of the most prestigious firms in consulting.

However, just because so many consultants and consulting entities have sullied the reputation of TCO by using it to guide their clients into making the purchases that the consultants wanted them to make, does not mean that the concept cannot be used by those who are **serious about performing** TCO analysis and benefitting from it. TCO is simply a tool and, as with any tool, can be used for positive or negative purposes. This is why reviewing the method by which the TCO was calculated as well as the source is equally important. The source of the TCO estimation must benefit from the decision, which the TCO estimation directs. There are no exceptions to these rules. When applying this standard, as I explain in Chapter 3: "The State of Enterprise TCO," it is difficult for implementing companies to get help with TCO. On the other hand, it is simple and easy to get rigged TCO analysis. For instance, most consulting companies that discuss TCO on topics such as outsourcing or software selection—or use it to compare one vendor to another—cannot be relied upon to provide objective information because they **benefit financially** from the implementing company's decision. For instance, if a major consulting company is providing outsourcing services, can the same consulting company's TCO estimation on outsourcing be trusted? Of course not, and in too many circumstances the concept of TCO has simply been to co-opt the approach as a marketing tool. This is why the "research" groups of all the major consulting companies are not taken seriously as real research entities, but are simply extensions of the marketing departments of those firms. In reviewing this "research," on numerous occasions, it was shocking to learn that many of the white papers and other published material are not even technically accurate, a good example of this being this paper by Booz Allen Hamilton.

http://www.scmfocus.com/inventoryoptimizationmultiechelon/2010/10/booz-allen-hamilton-misrepresents-inventory-optimization-in-white-papers/

To actually put a white paper on the Internet, when you lack the domain expertise to understand the topic of the paper, takes enormous hubris. It presumes that no one else will point this out.

The first rule of any TCO analysis—or, in fact, any analysis—is that the entity performing the analysis must not have a vested interest in its outcome. This fundamental rule is violated routinely in the enterprise software space, as explained in detail in the SCM Focus Book *Gartner and the Magic Quadrant: A Guide for Buyers, Vendors, and Investors.* An important defense against chicanery is improving one's knowledge of what goes into a TCO analysis. If what makes up a thorough TCO analysis were better understood, presenting a *faux* TCO analysis would be more difficult. While TCO analysis may be undermined from multiple dimensions and by multiple entities, it is very important to get TCO right; corporate purchases are more complex than consumer purchases. The second rule of any TCO analysis is that the entity performing the analysis must have the subject matter expertise in the subject—worked with it, implemented it, etc., that the TCO involves.

Objectives of the Book

This book hopes to explain how important TCO is and why the analysis of TCO should be performed in a better and more consistent manner. I also hope to add something new to the area of TCO—several of the observations made in this book are not generally discussed in published information on TCO. One of these observations is that the person or persons performing the analysis should have experience in the area for which the TCO is being performed. For example, I have worked very closely with enterprise software during my entire career. Any TCO analysis that I would perform for an area outside of my expertise—say purchasing an oil platform—would be of limited value unless I could tap the expertise of someone who had worked on multiple oil platforms for a number of years and who understood how oil platforms were installed, maintained, etc. TCO may be a financial analysis, but the easy part of the analysis is setting up the spreadsheet and doing the math. The difficult part is in the domain expertise to determine which assumptions to use; even people who are very experienced in a particular area can still benefit from objective input from others with similar expertise. For example, while I have estimated the TCO for many software categories in which I have direct implementation experience, I have also developed estimates for other enterprise software categories in which I do not have personal experience on implementations. When doing this, much more research is necessary. This means triangulating with people who have significant implementation know-how, and who can fill in some of the areas for which I have less knowledge. However, any analysis, which the analyst does not have direct experience working with, makes the analysis less reliable.

Here is the best rule of thumb: while there are similarities between all software projects, even implementations of the same software have discrepancies. These discrepancies are based upon the functionality being deployed and the client's level of preparedness for the application, and have caused some people to throw up their hands and say that TCO is not attainable. However, with sufficient effort, this challenge can be overcome. Even with a high forecast error, it is still of value to create a forecast. The key to dealing with complexity and variability is to keep doing the exercise. One way or another, either consciously or subconsciously, some assumptions are going to be made when it comes to decision-making. These assumptions can be investigated—resulting in a forecast that will have an error, or the analysis can be skipped, but then the assumptions will essentially be unanalyzed. Treating all applications as if they have the same TCO, or the same likelihood of being implemented successfully is simply not logical.

TCO analysis is often thought to be the province of strategy consultants or finance types. However, the most important qualification for performing a TCO analysis is not financial acumen. Rather, the qualifications are domain expertise for the product or service for which the TCO is being analyzed, some analytical capability, and most importantly, a lack of bias in the outcome of the decision that the TCO will influence.

Books and other Publications on Enterprise Software TCO

All SCM Focus Press books require a comprehensive literature review to be performed before beginning any new book. One of my favorite research quotations is from the highly respected RAND Corporation, a think tank based in sunny Santa Monica, California—a location not far from where I grew up and where I used to walk right by with my friend when I was in high school—at that time having no idea of the historically significant institution that I used to walk by on my lost surfing weekends. This is from RAND's "Standards for High Quality Research and Analysis" publication and makes the following statement regarding how its research references other work.

> *"A high-quality study cannot be done in intellectual isolation: It necessarily builds on and contributes to a body of research and analysis. The relationships between a given study and its predecessors should be rich and explicit. The study team's understanding of past research should be evident in many aspects of its work, from the way in which the problem is formulated and approached to the discussion of the findings and their implications. The team should take particular care to explain the ways in which its study agrees, disagrees, or otherwise differs importantly from previous studies. Failure to demonstrate an*

understanding of previous research lowers the perceived quality of a study, despite any other good characteristics it may possess."

In writing my other books, I have often found quite a lot of good reference material. I cannot say the same for the topic of TCO. As with my research into the benefits of ERP systems in *The Real Story Behind ERP: Separating Fact from Fiction*, most of the material published was low in details, had little evidence to support the contentions of the publications, and had a strong tendency to repeat conventional platitudes. I am not the first to notice this. A researcher who came before me noted this shortage of material. Back in 2003, Alan MacCormack, with Harvard University, compiled a study of fifty-five articles on TCO. He found that forty-two had **no data** and were categorized as informed speculation, one was a case study, nine projected the TCO for a specific firm, and three were used to report TCO for specific workloads. By the way, vendors sponsored two of these last three studies. Ten years after MacCormack's study, I essentially performed research of the literature, and can say that not much has changed in the intervening decade. I quote from Alan MacCormack below:

> *"As we can see, despite the widespread interest in evaluating TCO, many of the articles and studies that weigh in on the debate actually bring very little evidence to bear on the topic."*

I could not agree with Alan more.

There are **no books published** that address enterprise software TCO. This book is the first to address this topic, or should I say, the first to address it in English. There is actually one book on the cost of "industrial" software, written in Spanish called *Costo Total de Propieda: Estrategia en la Industria del Software*. I found it humorous that the only book on TCO for enterprise software was in Spanish, as it's the first time that has happened in any of the literature reviews I have performed for my books. I was a little surprised when I could not find a book on the topic for enterprise software, because I had heard the concept of TCO used occasionally on projects and had assumed TCO was a much more mature set of approaches than it really is. In fact, there are very few books on TCO overall—not simply a shortage of books on TCO as applied to enterprise software.

My Background and the Book's Focus and Orientation

I thought it important to talk about my background. I am an author and independent consultant who spent his career in advanced supply chain planning software. My career has provided me with exposure to not only supply chain software, but also to ERP, reporting, middleware and infrastructure software. I began performing TCO analysis several years ago because some of the assumptions I kept hearing on projects were not adding up. I work in an area that utilizes expensive applications; these applications cannot compete with applications from smaller vendors, both in terms of price and in terms of the actual features of the software. However, companies continue to make bad purchasing decisions based upon overly simplified concepts and the overestimation of costs, which were not all that significant to the TCO of the application. These TCO analyses were published at SCM Focus and have continued to be popular articles. They are still some of the few TCO analyses to be published in this software category. I was able to publish these articles—and to publish them in a complete form and to keep them up—primarily because I am an independent consultant. If I had published these articles and had been employed by a major consulting company that made its money from the application that performed poorly in the TCO analysis, I would have been forced to delete the articles. This is something that **must be recognized**: it is not merely problematic to get a straight story on TCO, or difficult to do the calculation, but also quite political. If the TCO estimation does not provide the "right answer," there is an overwhelming motivation to either not release the analysis or to alter it to meet the desired conclusion. TCO analysis leads to some decisions that benefit some company over others.

A focus of this book is to tell the true story about TCO and not skirt around the edges of the topic or talk about what "a *good idea TCO is*" in the abstract. This is a book for people who want to roll up their sleeves and do some quality TCO analysis, or at the very least, to understand how it works. This discussion of bias is a good lead-in to the next section.

How Writing Bias Is Controlled at SCM Focus and SCM Focus Press

Bias is a serious problem in the enterprise software field. Large vendors receive uncritical coverage of their products, and large consulting companies recommend the large vendors that have the resources to hire and pay consultants rather than the vendors with the best software for the client's needs.

At SCM Focus, we have yet to financially benefit from a company's decision to buy an application showcased in print, either in a book or on the SCM Focus website. This may change in the future as SCM Focus grows—but we have been writing with a strong viewpoint for years without coming into any conflicts of interest. SCM Focus has the most stringent rules related to controlling bias and restricting commercial influence of any information provider. These "writing rules" are provided in the link below:

   http://www.scmfocus.com/writing-rules/

If other information providers followed these rules, we would be able to learn about software without being required to perform our own research and testing for every topic.

Information about enterprise supply chain planning software can be found on the Internet, but this information is primarily promotional or written at such a high level that none of the important details or limitations of the application are exposed; this is true of books as well. When only one enterprise software application is covered in a book, one will find that the application works perfectly; the application operates as expected and there are no problems during the implementation to bring the application live. This is all quite amazing and quite different from my experience of implementing enterprise software. However, it is very difficult to make a living by providing objective information about enterprise supply chain software, especially as it means being critical at some point. I once remarked to a friend that SCM Focus had very little competition in providing untarnished information on this software category, and he said, "Of course, there is no money in it."

The Approach to the Book
By writing this book, I wanted to help people get exactly the information they need without having to read a lengthy volume. The approach to the book is

essentially the same as my previous books, and in writing this book I followed the same principles.

1. *Be direct and concise.* There is very little theory in this book and the math that I cover is simple. This book is focused on software and for most users and implementers of the software the most important thing to understand is conceptually what the software is doing.

2. *Based on project experience.* Nothing in the book is hypothetical; I have worked with it or tested it on an actual project. My project experience has led to my understanding a number of things that are not covered in typical supply planning books. In this book, I pass on this understanding to you.

The SCM Focus Site
As I am also the author of the SCM Focus site, http://www.scmfocus.com, the site and the book share a number of concepts and graphics. Furthermore, this book contains many links to articles on the site, which provide more detail on specific subjects.

Intended Audience
As I said previously, this is a book for people who want to roll up their sleeves and do some quality TCO analysis, or at the very least understand how TCO works. If you have any questions or comments on the book, please e-mail me at shaunsnapp@scmfocus.com.

Abbreviations
A listing of all abbreviations used throughout the book is provided at the end of the book.

Corrections
Corrections and updates, as well as reader comments, can be viewed in the comment section of this book's web page. Also, if you have comments or questions please add them to the following link:

http://www.scmfocus.com/scmfocuspress/it-decision-making-books/enterprise-software-tco/

CHAPTER 2

The Basics of TCO

Before we dive into the details of how TCO is performed and how it has influenced decision-making, let's start off with the absolute basics of TCO.

What is Total Cost of Ownership?

Total cost of ownership, or TCO, is the complete cost of owning something. TCO can be rearward looking—an accounting of what a purchase actually cost. However, in most cases a TCO analysis results in a forward projection or forecast. TCO for enterprise software is the overall sum of the costs of the four main TCO categories:

1. Software Cost

2. Hardware Cost

3. Implementation Cost

4. Maintenance Cost

The primary concept behind TCO is that often all costs are not considered or calculated when making purchasing decisions. The purchase of an automobile is a good example. If, for instance, a person were to budget all of their current excess discretionary income for a car and use its purchase price as a budgetary guideline, they would soon run into trouble because an automobile has ongoing additional costs such as maintenance. Anyone who has owned a car, a house, a boat, or any capital expense item would know that it is all too easy to overlook maintenance costs when making a purchase. How often have you heard a friend declare that if they had known the full cost of an item, they never would have purchased it in the first place?

The purchase price is referred to as an "explicit cost," meaning the cost is published, obvious, and easy to include when making a decision. However, a purchase implies many other costs, which may or may not be known at the time of purchase. Total cost of ownership attempts to combine all of the different categories of costs into one number and use that number for making decisions. TCO can change a decision about a purchase that, at first glance, may seem less expensive than other alternatives but in the end is actually more expensive.

TCO is discussed in the abstract but is rarely calculated in reality. If you think back upon all of the purchases you made throughout your life, how many of them included the TCO on the price tag, along with the actual purchase price? There is a good reason (or good reasons) for this and they go by the names of sales and marketing.

Sales and Marketing and TCO

The primary objective of sales and marketing is to increase sales. Sales decrease when customers come to understand the TCO of their purchases. Every purchase has a particular ratio: the ratio of the costs to its benefits. In the customer's mind, the lower this ratio (as this ratio is perceptual), the more likely it is that they will make a purchase. Sales and marketing "work their magic" by increasing the perceived benefit of a purchase while decreasing its perceived cost. Having the prospective customer place the purchase on a payment plan can further reduce the sting of the most explicit cost: the initial purchase price.

The last thing a company wants is for their prospective customers to know the total cost of an item. The one exception to this rule is if the vendor has a study that shows their product or service has a lower TCO than that of a competitor's product or service. Some software vendors create a white paper that shows the results of a TCO analysis within their software category, and lo and behold—on every occasion they, of course, have the lowest TCO! Even so, such advertisements of TCO in any context are rare.

Obviously, TCO analysis should be produced by an independent source and not the entity that is selling the item. TCO **is fundamentally a consumer concept, not a producer concept**. Therefore the consumer—or an entity with the consumer's or purchaser's interests at heart—should perform the research and publish the results of the TCO. There is a research company that does this, but they serve the consumer market rather than the corporate market. This company is Consumer Reports. They perform TCO for consumer items. Consumer Reports is in a good position to do this because they take no advertising from any producer and only make their money from consumer subscriptions. The following is a TCO estimation for automobile ownership.

> *"CR's calculations in seven common automotive categories show that the most expensive vehicle to run for five years is the Mercedes-Benz S550 at about $101,750. CR's calculated that the least expensive vehicle to run over five years was the Toyota Yaris with a manual transmission, at about $23,250.*
>
> *"One of the least expensive cars to own in our estimation is the small Honda Fit, which costs just over $5,300 a year to own for five years. It combines a relatively low purchase price with low depreciation, great fuel economy, excellent reliability, and fairly low maintenance and repair costs.*
>
> *"Paying more for a hybrid can save you money—as long as you choose the right hybrid. Most mainstream hybrids that aren't luxury or SUV models cost less to own over five years than their less expensive conventional counterparts. (Two exceptions are the Chevrolet Volt and Honda Insight. It takes six or seven years, respectively, to make up the added purchase price in fuel savings for those cars.)"* — Consumer Reports

These reports are valuable because they provide very actionable intelligence that consumers can use to make informed purchasing decisions and to avoid cars that have hidden maintenance costs. Consumer Reports is one of the few media entities that can say they are not swayed by vendor influence because they put a number of restrictions in place that are designed to counteract vendor influence. Consumer Reports goes to the extent of actually purchasing the products they review rather than relying upon free samples—which is how almost all media entities operate that review products. This, of course, puts the media entity into the debt of the vendor, as well as allows the vendor to "adjust" the reviewed product so that it is perfect—and different from the experience that the normal consumer would receive.

TCO Versus ROI

It is important not to confuse TCO with its close financial cousin: return on investment (ROI). Below is a definition of how TCO and ROI are related to one another.

> *"TCO analysis is not a complete cost benefit analysis, however. TCO pays no attention to many kinds of business benefits that result from acquisitions, projects, or initiatives, such as increased sales revenues, faster information access, improved operational capability, improved competitiveness, or improved product quality. When TCO is the primary focus in decision support, it is assumed that such benefits are more or less the same for all decision options, and that management choices differ only in cost."* — Encyclopedia of Business Terms and Methods

In actuality, few software products provide identical benefits, and the more complex the product, the more variability between each alternative's return on investment (ROI). The simplest items—commodities—are the easiest to compare, precisely because their properties (in this case physical properties) are **uniform**. This is why silver, tin, grain, cotton, etc. can be sold on commodity exchanges. In contrast, enterprise software is complex; each application has different implications for how well the software meets the business requirements in terms of functionality, effectiveness of the user interface, ease of integration with other applications, amount of support needed, and hardware requirements—and those are just the major items. Frequently the variability or score of these different items is unknown during the software selection process.

How ROI and TCO are connected.

TCO is the base value for ROI: it is the "I" in ROI. A TCO must be calculated before an ROI can be calculated. ROI is the formalized analysis of the universal ratio between costs and benefits, which I referred to previously, and is focused on both the revenue and the costs of an investment. Unlike TCO, ROI takes into account the benefits from an acquisition. This is brought up in a quote from Ian Campbell of Nucleus Research:

> *"The real problem with TCO is that it's a metric that can't be used to make a buying decision. TCO assesses costs without regard for the benefits. We buy based on value, and I'd challenge you to think of an item you purchase in your daily lives based solely on lowest costs."*

While this is true, the ROI is based partially upon the TCO. Therefore, while I don't propose that TCO is the end point of the analysis, it is important to know the TCO before moving on to other analyses. Secondly, the ROI of enterprise software is quite difficult because it means estimating the financial returns from software, which is an extremely complex endeavor. Calculation of ROI is complicated by the fact that the specific areas of functionality that will be leveraged by the company must be estimated, and then the net benefit of that functionality must be projected. This is the only way that we know of providing a differential ROI between competing applications in a software selection. It is interesting to read articles about ROI, and after reading through them just to find essentially nothing explained of how to estimate ROI. There is actually far less published on ROI than TCO. In one way this can be seen as curious as so much is spent on enterprise software, but it is considerably less curious when one appreciates how difficult it is to calculate an ROI. And, in fact, once you dig into the detail of ROI estimations, it turns out that there is not much there. Furthermore, there are both explicit and implicit benefits to software, and the ROI estimations that we have evaluated will bring up the explicit or the "hard" benefits only, as it is often considered "too difficult" to ascribe a number to the implicit or "soft" benefits.

Therefore, instead of producing ROI estimates, Software Decisions applies a rating system to the application, which is used in conjunction with the TCO estimate. These are the following:

1. A Functionality Score

2. An Implement-ability Score

3. A Usability Score

4. A Maintainability Score

This results in a composite score, which the client can weigh toward the factors that are most important to them, or they can simply apply an even twenty-five percent weight to each score. This still allows the value of the software to be estimated, but without the necessity for an ROI calculation. The combination of the TCO and the application's composite score captures the multiple dimensions of the application and is an effective approach for making a determination on software.

A company typically looks for **the highest ROI, and simply the lowest TCO**. For example, an application with a higher TCO than a competing application can also have a higher ROI, making the product with the higher TCO the preferred choice.

Net Present Value and TCO

Financial analysts, and anyone who has taken a finance course, are familiar with performing net present value calculations (NPV). NPV discounts the future benefits and future costs into present day numbers through the introduction of some interest rate, often the company's cost of capital. We do not add net present value calculations along with TCO estimations. If we did, it would shift the emphasis somewhat to applications that have lower up-front costs, such as SaaS solutions that charge for software on the basis of a subscription and have low implementation costs. However, the TCO advantage of SaaS solutions based on TCO in comparison to on-premises applications is already overwhelming and would simply show further differences.

NPV can be calculated once the discount rate the company wants to use is applied, but in most cases it will not make a difference between competing applications within the same software category, or software categories that are competing with one another for funding. And actually, it's rare to include NPV in the TCO estimation. NPV is the most accurate approach, but TCO estimations tend to contain so many assumptions that NPV tends to further complicate the analysis (as well as the reader's ability to understand the analysis). Secondly, as I will discuss in more detail, when the TCO methodologies are normalized (that is, adjusted to be comparable), then TCO from different sources can be used quite effectively; this improves the overall usability of TCO for the broadest decision-making. But, if other sources of TCO **do not use** NPV, it does not make a lot of sense to use NPV for one's own TCO estimation. Thirdly, TCO is essentially a comparative exercise. When TCO is calculated and a company bases a software, hardware, or services purchase on that TCO analysis, they do not actually have to **cut a check** for the TCO amount when they make the purchase. The TCO estimation is a guideline for how the future costs should work out. Therefore, as long as the various TCO estimations have a similar basis, or are normalized, precise adjustments such as NPV are not necessary.

CHAPTER 3

The State of Enterprise TCO

Correct TCO analysis requires effort; getting into the real detail of the costs and benefits of applications requires a combination of first-hand implementation experience as well as the analytical ability to perform the analysis. This analysis should be built from a level of detail such that the TCO flows naturally from the more thorough analysis.

> *"Total cost of operations (TCO)-based financial analysis is held up as the gold standard for technology investment justification, **but most firms don't have the rigor to apply the discipline to their environment.**"* — Forrester

The more we have reviewed TCO calculations from various external sources, the less we find exists behind them. This is reminiscent of accounting auditing. On the surface, the signature of an accounting firm on an annual report looks impressive. The accounting firm is stating that the books were prepared in a way consistent with generally accepted accounting principles (GAAP). In fact, it's all very impressive until you actually look at what the audit checked.

For example let's say that a company mines, warehouses and distributes gold. Let's further say that in their annual report they have one hundred bars of gold worth roughly $150 million. The gold company now needs an auditor to sign off on their books. So auditor XYZ is paid a fee to check the gold company's books. The auditor reviews the arithmetic, and notes that at a price of $1.5 million per bar combined with the fact that the company reports having one hundred bars, that lo and behold $1.5 million × 100 is in fact $150 million. The auditor **does not go to the warehouse to check if the gold bars are actually there**. Instead the auditor merely checks the client's **arithmetic** and whether the company followed the accounting rules. Let's say the gold company reported ninety-eight gold bars in inventory on December 30th of the tax year, and then one hundred gold bars on January 2nd. Because the gold company did not have the two extra gold bars in its warehouse in the calendar year for which the auditor is signing the annual report, the auditor may say that it is not consistent with GAAP, and would tell the gold company to change the number of gold bars reported in its annual report from one hundred to ninety-eight.

Auditing produces an illusion where it seems that it checks **much more than it actually does,** and therefore an auditor's signature means much more than it actually should. In reality, accounting firms have all types of legal escapes when their audits don't check out. When a company is caught for some type of accounting irregularity (or for out-and-out fraud), the auditing firm backs off of its promises to provide assurance, and simply states that they did not know this or that detail. This is of course an easy argument to buy once you realize that they don't do much but check arithmetic and that the "books" are consistent with GAAP.

Public companies must have a well-known auditing company sign their annual reports, even though auditing is just a surface analysis. Thus auditing firms are able to make a nice amount of money for little work. Furthermore, because the company (and not the stockholders or investors) pays the auditor, the auditor does not **want to look too deeply,** as their interests are aligned with the people who want to obscure the truth and not with the people who want to know. If the auditing company will not play ball, there are always other auditors who can be given the business, although this is rarely necessary as in most cases the auditors will sign the annual report with some slight adjustments.[2]

The same concept is at work with bond rating. Bond rating is now well known because of the 2008 financial crisis, which brought to light the fact that the bond ratings were a farce. When rating agencies analyzed how the bond rating agencies gave AAA ratings to so many horribly risky bonds (their highest rating meant that it was investment grade and essentially had no chance of default), it turned out that there was nothing behind their ratings. During US Senate hearings on this topic, the rating agencies stated that their ratings—which are marketed on their website and in their marketing literature as serious analysis—are really just their "opinions," and argued (rather ludicrously) that their right to distribute false information is protected by the first amendment to the US Constitution.

> *"In announcing the case, Eric Holder, America's attorney general, said that S&P had misrepresented the credit risk of the securities it rated and pretended to act objectively. 'S&P's desire for increased revenue and market share,' Mr. Holder asserted, 'led it to favour the interests of investment banks issuing securities over those of investors.'"*— The Economist

As a result of shallow analysis, the US has constant bubbles, which then pop and cause great damage to the economy. Every few years the insubstantial nature of the analysis that is thought generally to help minimize risk in the financial industry comes to light whenever the asset bubbles pop and investors get hurt. Few are punished. Some industry-written insubstantial reforms are passed and the process repeats itself. The sad fact is that regardless of the area—auditing, bond rating, enterprise software analysis, and advice from either consulting companies or IT analysts—it is extremely difficult to find unbiased and competent analysis.

---

[2] A problem with auditing is that the major accounting companies also have consulting arms. The auditing company is not just playing for the audit side of the business, but wants to sell consulting services as well. If given more consulting services, they can be motivated to look even further away than they do ordinarily. This was the issue with Enron, which was giving Anderson Consulting roughly $1 million per month in consulting revenue. The audit side of the business was told to do what was required to keep the money flowing.

The Relationship to TCO

If these stories are not news to you, you should feel right at home when analyzing TCO. The same superficial orientation that permeates financial auditing and bond ratings is also prevalent in TCO analysis, and this shallow analysis, which is part of software selection, results in poor software decisions. In fact, incomplete or incorrectly performed TCO is behind poor decisions ranging from overinvestments in ERP to outsourcing decisions. The algorithm for how this works is quite simple.

1. A trend will become popular.

2. People make decisions based upon the trend without a thorough analysis of what migrating to this trend will mean for the company in reality.

3. Information will surface about problems with the trend, and excuses will be made for the unanalyzed trend. Articles will surface about how to mitigate the issues that come with implementing the new trend.

What never seems to occur is a detailed analysis of whether the trend or idea had any validity in the first place. My research into TCO and other topics such as ERP systems—as is explained in the SCM Focus Press book, *The Real Story Behind ERP: Separating Fact from Fiction,* has revealed something I have suspected for some time:

1. *Non-Evidence Based Decision Making:* Many trends have no evidence for the benefits they supposedly provide, and the marketing is often far ahead of the research.

2. *Poor to Nonexistent Analysis:* Decision makers in companies are simply not doing their homework, and are making decisions by simply looking around at whatever anyone else is doing.

3. *Advisor Bias:* Advisors who put their own interests ahead of their clients' interests constantly mislead executive decision makers.

Another interesting factor is how companies hide their bad decisions. You hardly ever read about companies that make bad software selections and fail in implementations, as they do whatever they can to cover up the stories. Instead the implementation itself may be criticized. But certainly uninformed decision making—both in terms of the software selected, as well as the implementation partner are greatly to blame. I have arrived at a number of projects to perform a post mortem, and upon reviewing the sales documentation and talking to the executives about what they were pitched, there was, in most cases, ample evidence to know that the project was not going to be successful, before the software was ever purchased. The only time one tends to hear about the details behind all of these stories is when the project goes so horribly wrong that a lawsuit is filed, as in the example of Marin County versus Deloitte, which is covered in the following articles.

http://www.scmfocus.com/sapprojectmanagement/2012/02/deloittes-legal-intimidation-of-marin-county-and-what-can-be-learned-from-it/

http://www.scmfocus.com/sapprojectmanagement/2012/02/has-deloitte-bought-off-someone-inside-your-organization-as-they-did-with-marin-county/

The reasons for this is because a court case requires filing court documents and this means disclosure. This is one of the few times that the truth actually comes out. While on one hand, bad software selections and implementations are hushed up, successful software implementations are typically discussed proudly and openly and the success is explained to journalists. All of the information that is released is **done with a keen eye toward the impact on the stock price.** And increasing stock prices mean manipulating the information that is released to Wall Street. Therefore, much like the floor of a casino (where the winning slots make a lot of noise and the losing slots are quiet) the positive observations are greatly over-estimated and over-emphasized.

Why (Some) Software Vendors Do Not Want Accurate TCO (or ROI) Calculated

I did not think I would have to include this section in the book because it's fairly obvious, but on the other hand, it's important that the issue does not go unaddressed. Software vendors with applications that have a high TCO do not want accurate TCO estimates for using its software. For example, software vendors that do not offer SaaS solutions also do not want TCO calculated. TCO research at Software Decisions shows that consistently, the TCO for the exact same application, when delivered as SaaS, is at least half as much as the on-premises version, and often less than half of the on-premises version. The cost advantages occur in an area that is **consistently underrated** by almost all TCO analyses that I have reviewed, which is the internal cost of support and maintenance. Let's take a look into SaaS as an example of why many vendors want to supress TCO estimation. With SaaS delivered solutions, while the internal support requirement does not go away—it is greatly reduced. The software vendor has full access to the system at all times as they host it. In fact the widespread adoption of SaaS most likely will transform internal IT in the coming decades, with much of the employment moving from internal IT departments and toward the software vendors. The cost and service advantages are large, with SaaS delivered applications being a much lower percentage of the market for enterprise software than it should be.

Not enough businesses are aware of the cost and quality differentials between SaaS and on-premise applications. In fact, in a study by IFS, only around twenty-two of the respondents stated that they were either "Familiar" or "Very Familiar" with SaaS.[3] There are challenges to overcome, particularly the necessity to standardize SaaS contracts to prevent the software vendors from selling their clients' data, mining it, or otherwise violating their customer's privacy in the way that Google and Facebook habitually do.

---

[3] Strangely, in this study cost was listed as a **disadvantage** to SaaS, which is the exact opposite of our TCO findings. Consistent with the growth of the largest SaaS software vendor, Salesforce, CRM was listed as the most common software category that was used in the SaaS delivery method.

Software Vendors Faking Enthusiasm for TCO

While most software vendors hide their pricing information, all software vendors still like to talk about TCO in the abstract.[4] Being in favor of TCO is like saying you are in favor of the American flag or apple pie; you're in favor of "goodness." You can't actually find anyone who opposes TCO in principle. But the devil is in the details. As long as nothing is quantified or the TCO studies are rigged, all vendors can say they have the lowest TCO. Most software vendors are not only against publishing TCO estimations, but are even against publishing pricing information for their applications on their websites.

The big vendors that would score poorly on TCO have plenty of resources to calculate TCO, but don't. It's like the mutual fund industry, they know the hidden fees in their mutual funds—but they are not going to tell you.[5] For example, SAP has the highest TCO in every application category that is analyzed at our companion site, Software Decisions—and not by a small margin.[6] The degree to which SAP has higher costs is explained fully in the book *Replacing Big ERP: Breaking the Big ERP Habit with Best-of-Breed Applications at a Fraction of the Cost*, and when we explain the large cost differential of SAP's TCO, SAP's comments regarding the importance of TCO are put in perspective. The last thing

---

[4] The problem with hiding pricing information is that it is used as a control technique by software vendors in order to pry information from the buyers. It also greatly lengthens the process of finding out the pricing information and reduces the comparability of applications. In order to function efficiently, markets require published price information. There are some laws in the US on this topic for consumer products, but not for products purchased by corporations. On several occasions vendors have sent me non-disclosure agreements (NDA) that covered **pricing** information. However, this is a misuse of the NDA legal concept, as NDAs are designed to protect proprietary information—technical information, software intellectual property—and not pricing information. The legal phraseology implied that I could be sued for sharing pricing information with a third party if it damaged the company's business. However, wouldn't any sharing of pricing information, unless the software vendors were the low cost provider "damage their business?" Pricing information is part of what makes markets work and should be published.

[5] There is a very interesting story about the lack of quantification of fees in the mutual fund industry, which has important connections to TCO but in a different realm. *"These include (401k) fees to cover the costs of advertising the plans and the companies who run them, fees to pay various investment managers of the funds in the plan, even fees to cover the costs of buying and selling the underlying stocks and bonds in which retirement accounts are invested. These fees, however, are taken "off the top" of investment returns or share prices—in other words, the rates of return and share prices reported to you in account statements and plan documents are post-fee. Because of this, retirement and bank account statements contain no evidence of these fees, and thus accountholders generally have no inkling how much all of this costs them."* — The Retirement Savings Drain: The Hidden and Excessive Costs of 401(k)s.

[6] Software Decisions is available at http://www.softwaredecisions.org.

either SAP or any of the major consulting companies want is for the **actual** TCO of SAP to be known. Oracle is in a similar TCO category.

Well, if the mega vendors don't want TCO to be known, how about the smaller vendors that tend to have much lower TCOs? Certainly they would want their TCO to be published as widely as possible right? Interestingly, the smaller best-of-breed vendors often do not allocate resources to calculating TCO.

There is also the realization that the numbers produced by the software vendors themselves will be taken with a grain of salt. It is certainly not difficult to find examples of software vendors creating false financial estimates for their clients in order to promote sales. I used to work for one of these companies and witnessed this firsthand (although I am happy to say I never participated in or supported this). The software vendor i2 Technologies offered something called a *Strategic Opportunity Assessment* (SOW), which estimated the financial implications of using its software.

> *"Another company, whose i2 deployment was two years behind schedule because of problems with i2 software, told Nucleus the following 'I2 did an ROI calculation for us during the sales process...it was very positive. But based upon our experience now, we will [independently] evaluate ROI in the future.'"* — Nucleus Research

How any company could actually believe a TCO or ROI study developed by a software vendor and which is part of a vendor's sales process, is...well, strange.[7] In a surreal turn, this company also priced their software based upon this value estimation. Talk about a conflict of interest! The following quote from Nucleus Research is educational:

> *"One customer, that is still cited on the i2 Web site (2003) as a success story but stopped using i2 more than a year ago, told Nucleus: 'What*

---

[7] Regardless of their actual quality, when I worked at this company, these SOWs were quite popular. Not to be outdone, I have created my own SOW and ROI for this book. I predict this book will save any companies that follow its advice roughly 1 billion dollars. So a 15% fee for that cost saving is reasonable. Please make your checks out for $150 million to SCM Focus Press.

killed the ROI was the fact that i2 priced their modules based on an ROI calculation that they themselves estimated during the sales process. (i2 stated) that this would lead to $40 million in benefits. There are definitely benefits to the solution, but their pricing is too high. Sometime, I should take the time to contact i2 and say you really need to look at your pricing.'"

Some vendors still produce TCO calculations and at SCM Focus we have analyzed a number of these TCO calculations. In fact, we have used some of these estimations for our own estimations and have found some good and some bad in how they were put together. Several of the most obvious issues are listed below:

1. **We have yet to come across a true "TCO" produced by a vendor.** While a few have been accurate in several respects, they did not estimate the client's cost of either working on the implementation or maintaining the application. However, the TCO is literally that; it must be inclusive of the entirety of costs to bring the application into the company and to keep it running, and even to decommission the application. I have certainly appreciated the work put in by software vendors to estimate some of the costs, but it is confusing to see "TCO" in a publication's title and then read the following *"...does—NOT—include analyst costs, IT costs, local data management costs, etc."* One could imagine the following riddle: *"When is a TCO not a TCO? When it does not include all costs."*

2. **Vendors have a strong tendency to underestimate the duration of the software implementation.** When I review actual implementations, they are much longer than estimated. It may certainly be true that the application could be installed as quickly as estimated in a laboratory environment, but companies are not laboratories. Some vendors (other than those like SAP and Oracle, both of which have business models of long implementations due to the needs of the consulting companies to which they outsource their consulting), will complain that the client is really what holds up the implementation. This is a bit like a doctor complaining that if only patients had medical degrees, he or she could see many more patients and get through the day faster. It's simply not relevant to the question of duration estimation. The following statement is included on the

TCO questionnaire that we give to vendors: *"Please use historical timelines rather than 'optimal scenario' timelines."* Therefore, the knowledge level of the client and the time required for knowledge transfer must be estimated, along with all of the other realities of projects. Another example of this is integration. IT departments are slow to respond with extract creation. This was true when I began working in IT back in 1997 and it is still true today. Many integration estimates provided by vendors do not include the time for the IT department to create the extracts to feed the pre-written adapter. A vendor may have a very nice adapter, but that does not change the fact that extracts must be written.[8]

Why Consulting Companies Do Not Want Accurate TCO Calculated

Behind many poor decisions is a lack of proper TCO analysis, many consulting companies are also behind poor decisions. Consulting companies don't share the economic benefit of their clients' good decisions, and therefore are not incentivized to promote good decision-making on the part of their clients. Instead they are incentivized purely by billing hours. And increasing billing means introducing things that the company does not currently have or does do not currently do. As I previously stated, a lack of proper TCO has been partially responsible for the overuse of both ERP and outsourcing—two trends that have greatly enriched the bottom lines of the major consulting companies. Whatever they can make a lot of money on, an army of partners is lined up ready to tell any client that they should be doing that thing.

Consulting companies make quite a lot of money from outsourcing. Therefore, they propose that outsourcing has a low TCO compared to the cost of hiring internal resources. In my experience, outsourcing has had a devastating effect on the IT organizations of companies that outsource. People who work in companies that

---

[8] I have continually run into this problem of accurate implementation estimations, whether working for or outside of software vendors. When I worked for a software vendor, I had constant debates with software salespeople who—although never having worked on an implementation themselves—felt qualified to provide estimates to clients regarding how long implementations would take. When the implementation team shows up, usually they must adjust the implementation duration estimates that were given to the client (particularly if the implementation project manager was never consulted prior to providing the estimate, which can happen). During an internal presentation to salespeople, one salesperson stated that the company was moving toward "two-week implementations." Typical implementations for this software were in the range of four to eight months.

outsourced portions of their IT support are too familiar with the ticket-based approach to service, where the outsourced service organization simply focuses on opening and closing tickets (which is how they are measured) rather than getting to the bottom of issues. It is well known that outsourcing IT support dramatically reduces a company's IT capabilities, and actually undermines their software and hardware investments. However, outsourcing of IT support continues unabated as it allows CIOs to claim "cost savings." These are explicit cost savings mind you, because an evaluation of the **TCO of the outsourcing decision would show a very different story**. One would find a lower utilization of the software that the company purchased, and efficiency losses throughout the entire company as more people spend more time with computer and software problems.

It is important to evaluate the incentives of consulting companies when looking at their recommendations. For instance, Indian consulting/outsourcing companies like Tata, Wipro and Infosys began in the US market primarily getting companies to outsource US roles to India. Their primary comparative advantage was and is **access** to large number of inexpensive overseas resources. The more that the US and Europe outsourced, the more money these companies made. The magazine *CIO* even had an explanation of how to properly lay off US employees, but not before extracting the information you need from them.[9] Another issue often not considered is the employee turnover at outsourcing firms, as is described by *CIO* in the quote below:

> *"Another productivity killer is high turnover at offshore vendors. Attrition rates climb as high as thirty-five percent in India, according to the National Association of Software and Service Companies. 'Unless you can somehow address that in your contract, you're paying for someone to learn your product and then they're gone,' Zupnick says. Turnover can cost an additional one percent to two percent."* — CIO

---

[9] *"Laying off American employees as a result of your offshore contract poses other sometimes unanticipated costs. To begin with, you have to pay many of those workers severance and retention bonuses. 'You need to keep employees there long enough to share their knowledge with their Indian replacements,' Zupnick explains. 'People think if they give generous retention bonuses it will destroy the business proposition. They cut corners because they want quick payback. But then they lose the people that can help with the transition and incur the even bigger cost of not doing the transition right.'"* — CIO

One issue that is not brought up often is that the way much of the IT outsourcing is unsustainable. Outsourcing conditions overseas are often so poor that they push individuals to the limit until they quit to find a new job. The initial costs are easy to calculate, but creating a TCO means estimating the turnover and the relearning that must take place at the offshore vendors. On one project we were supposed to transition knowledge to Wipro consultants; however the pay and working conditions were so poor that the Wipro consultants would routinely quit, so the knowledge transfer was minimal. However, for some time CSC, Accenture, Deloitte, etc., have all developed enormous IT outsourcing practices. All of these companies write articles on the TCO of outsourcing, which sound objective but are **essentially marketing brochures for their outsourcing services**. This again is the problem when the advisor is also the provider of a service.

Why (Even) Purchasing Companies May Not Want TCO Calculated

It's easy to beat up on consulting companies for not looking out for their clients' interests. Many times I have personally seen consulting companies deliberately mislead their clients, and I have been pressured by consulting partners to participate in misleading the client. Furthermore, this is very well known among people with experience in the consulting field. In consulting it's all about the billing hours. Billing hours control compensation, who gets promoted, who make partner and who stays a partner. Therefore, it's not surprising that consulting companies do not want TCO calculated for things they benefit financially from selling. However, the sad fact is that many buying/implementing companies also do not want TCO calculated. In order to understand why, it's necessary to understand the loose connection between the interests of the executive decision makers in companies versus the interests of shareholders. Secondly, it's important to understand how companies are measured.

Why IT Analysts Don't Want TCO Calculated

Gartner, the IT analyst company, was one of the first entities to market around the idea of TCO. However, Gartner never did much more than stay at the conceptual level. The likely reason for this is fairly simple: if Gartner had actually calculated the TCO for the applications it reviewed, it would have given all the "wrong" answers. I quote from the SCM Focus Press book *Gartner and the Magic Quadrant: A Guide for Buyers, Vendors and Investors*.

"Gartner also tends to push buyers toward more expensive solutions. This higher expense is not only for software, but also for services. For instance, I work as an SAP consultant, and SAP consultants are some of the most expensive resources in IT. One aspect of the cost is the hourly billing rate, which is high. Another aspect is that SAP software is complicated to install, so SAP projects tend to be quite long."

Not only does Gartner not disclose its income from vendors for "technology advisement services," but also does whatever it can to prevent buyers from knowing that it takes any income from software vendors. When someone who knows how the system works brings up this issue, Gartner points to the fact that they have an ombudsman, so none of the quite significant revenues they get from vendors has any influence on their ratings. However, this "ombudsman" follows none of the rules of a traditional ombudsman, and as the complaint process is completely hidden from view, the ombudsman cannot be considered an objective arbiter. This in fact was the exact charge in the lawsuit brought about by a software vendor named ZL Technologies, as explained in the following quotation.

"Gartner currently has an employee act as ombudsman to handle disagreements. The conflict of interest is self-evident in the way ZL's concerns were summarily dismissed with little supporting evidence. There is a crying need to establish an impartial ombudsman similar to those found in public media, in order to ensure purchasers that they are receiving impartial analysis."

My conclusion, which is the exact same conclusion of every director or vice-president of marketing at a best-of-breed vendor with whom I have discussed this topic, is that payments from vendors influence Gartner's ratings **substantially**. Not **one** best-of-breed vendor I have ever spoken to thought Gartner was an unbiased source of information on software vendors. Not one.

The system is rigged in favor of vendors that pay the most—and the vendors that can afford to pay Gartner the most are those with the highest license fees. Therefore, one of Gartner's main roles is to guide buyers to both the most expensive TCO software solutions in the market, as well as to the most expensive consulting companies. Gartner could not perform an honest TCO analysis for any of the software categories that it covers without alienating its biggest vendor customers. Therefore, Gartner has no interest in TCO beyond discussing it as a general principle.

The Warner Brothers Example

One very well known media company provides a perfect example of how not performing a proper TCO estimation can result in making a poor decision.

Warner Brothers made the decision to outsource its IT department back in 2008. Warner Brothers itself did not want to outsource, but was forced to do so by their parent company Time Warner. Leading up to this decision, no studies of any kind were undertaken and certainly no true TCO was performed to inform this decision. Instead estimates, taken from Cap Gemini, were used to justify the change and explain the expected cost savings. Of course Cap Gemini was going to take over part of the outsourced workforce, so they had a powerful bias in proposing that outsourcing would save Time Warner a great deal of money. These cost savings were believed (by Time Warner at least, if not Warner Brothers), and the program was announced to the media in January of 2009. Eight hundred employees, or ten percent of the Warner Brothers work force at the time, would be outsourced.

> *"The 800 positions break down as follows: 200 open positions around the world; 300 outsourced (with a third being offered employment opportunities with Cap Gemini and continue to be based in Burbank), and 300 lay-offs."* — Warner Bros. Announces 800 Layoffs

This initiative was, in part, a PR stunt intended to boost the stock price. Warner Brothers had experienced some down quarters, and it needed to do something to increase the stock price. Outsourcing communicated to the financial markets that Warner Brothers was "doing something" to reduce its costs.

Information from inside of Warner Brothers indicates that the outsourcing program was a failure, and Warner Brothers has since brought many of these jobs back in-house **because the quality of the IT support that was received was**

so poor. However, Warner Brothers did not make this announcement because it had no PR value. Wall Street wants to hear about outsourcing stories—not insourcing. Warner Brothers would in effect be admitting that their program had failed. And Wall Street analysts—who know less than nothing about running a business and do not consider the effect of the quality of IT support on the operations of a business—merely view various announcements through a conformist lens: outsourcing good, insourcing bad. Analysts would have penalized Warner Brothers because after all, "insourcing simply increases costs."[10] Again, all information that is released must have a positive impact on the stock price because to a large extent the executives are compensated in stock. In fact, responsiveness to the financial markets is a big reason why initiatives are taken, and has very little to do with improving the condition of the company.

In part, companies implement systems like ERP and initiatives like outsourcing not because there is any evidence that they benefit the company, but because the company needs to demonstrate to outsiders that they are doing "all the right things." The financial analysts who evaluate stocks have no experience with ERP and have never participated in IT outsourcing, so they do not know whether these things have any inherent value either way—but they do know what is trendy and

---

[10] Here is the logic for the statement that Wall Street analysts know less than nothing about running a business. If one knew nothing—then one would not jump to conclusions either way when a company makes an announcement regarding an initiative. Wall Street analysts think they know, but primarily interpret information that is released—and much of it false by the way—based upon what they have been told is beneficial to businesses, and much of this is simply based upon what they have heard to be beneficial, which is often whatever is short term and trendy. So if a company lays off workers—although it may undermine the company's ability to serve customers in the future—that is seen as positive. *"See, the company is getting lean and mean."* If a company announces a Six Sigma program or something else trendy, the Wall Street analyst—not having participated in this program—will often assume it is something good. This type of simpleminded thinking is extremely destructive to the overall economic system as executive decision makers are trying to appeal to people who do not themselves know. Imagine a beauty pageant where all the judges are blind. Secondly, the connection between corporate announcements and what is actually successfully implemented in a company is dubious. Wall Street's ability to see beyond a short-term short cut to cost cutting is also quite dubious. The ability of Wall Street to look out for the long-term interests of the company is very weak, and for what is good or at least societally sustainable is non-existent. Certainly, there is little doubt that if slavery were re-legalized, the stock market would go through the roof. Just imagine the profits! This desire to impress Wall Street has lead to outsourcing manufacturing, even when the financial case for it is weak.

topical. These "right things" change depending upon what happens to be trendy at the time.

When I discussed this book with a colleague, who is quite experienced in these matters, he questioned whether a service to provide TCO analysis would have a market. He stated:

> *"Who would be the market? It's not the consulting companies, because any company that offered honest TCO evaluation services would be their enemy. It's also not the purchasing companies, because this type of information would interfere with their stock options and their ability to get rich."*

Other TCO Failures

As I have explained, TCO is barely performed in any shape or form in IT for either software selection or other IT decisions such as outsourcing, and when it is done, it is usually done poorly. However, I do not want to give the impression that this issue is specific to IT. Companies have major problems performing TCO, and these problems extend to all manner of areas. One is manufacturing outsourcing, where many outsourcing decisions were made by comparing part costs and not by performing a TCO analysis. Many companies compared the direct part cost between the US and China, found a lower cost of between twenty-five and forty percent, but did not consider other costs! Costs such as longer lead times, reduction in supply chain flexibility, loss of control over the supply chain, bottlenecks, as well as many other costs needed to be evaluated before the outsourcing decision was made. The following graphic from Archstone Consulting shows all of the different cost categories that must be analyzed in manufacturing outsourcing.

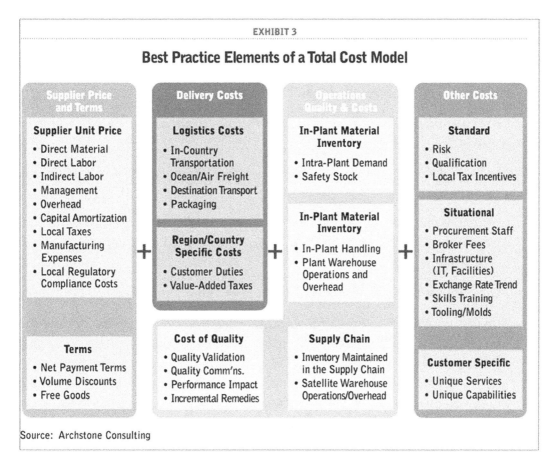

EXHIBIT 3

Best Practice Elements of a Total Cost Model

Supplier Price and Terms	Delivery Costs	Operations Quality & Costs	Other Costs
Supplier Unit Price • Direct Material • Direct Labor • Indirect Labor • Management • Overhead • Capital Amortization • Local Taxes • Manufacturing Expenses • Local Regulatory Compliance Costs	**Logistics Costs** • In-Country Transportation • Ocean/Air Freight • Destination Transport • Packaging	**In-Plant Material Inventory** • Intra-Plant Demand • Safety Stock	**Standard** • Risk • Qualification • Local Tax Incentives
	Region/Country Specific Costs • Customer Duties • Value-Added Taxes	**In-Plant Material Inventory** • In-Plant Handling • Plant Warehouse Operations and Overhead	**Situational** • Procurement Staff • Broker Fees • Infrastructure (IT, Facilities) • Exchange Rate Trend • Skills Training • Tooling/Molds
Terms • Net Payment Terms • Volume Discounts • Free Goods	**Cost of Quality** • Quality Validation • Quality Comm'ns. • Performance Impact • Incremental Remedies	**Supply Chain** • Inventory Maintained in the Supply Chain • Satellite Warehouse Operations/Overhead	**Customer Specific** • Unique Services • Unique Capabilities

Source: Archstone Consulting

Most companies that performed manufacturing outsourcing were not interested in getting to this level of detail. It was far easier to simply compare part costs and assume everything else would stay about the same. This is what passes for analysis at many companies. Based on a 2009 survey, Archstone Consulting estimated that sixty percent of manufacturers ignored twenty percent or more of the costs of offshoring.

Many factors are left out of the TCO analysis of manufacturing outsourcing, including the following.

- *"Currency Fluctuations: Last year's invoice of $100,000 could be $140,000 today.*

- *Lack of Managing an Offshore Contract: Underestimating the people, process, and technology required to manage an outsourcing contract.*

- *Design Changes: Language barriers make it difficult to get design changes understood and implemented.*

- *Quality Problems: Substitution of lower grade or different materials than specified is a common problem.*

- *Legal Liabilities: Offshore vendors refuse to participate in product warrantees or guarantees.*

- *Travel Expenses: One or more visits to an offshore vendor can dissipate cost savings.*

- *Cost of Transition: Overlooking the time and effort required to do things in a new way. It takes from three months to a year to complete the transition to an offshore vendor.*

- *Poor Communication: Communication is extremely complex and burdensome.*

- *Intellectual Property: Foreign companies, particularly Chinese, are notorious for infringing on IP rights without legal recourse for American companies."*
— Michele Nash-Hoff

Considering the numerous accountants and financial experts that work in so many companies, the rudimentary nature of how companies make cost decisions can be shocking.

> *"Accountants deal with hard costs such as material costs, material overhead costs, labor costs, labor overhead costs, quality costs, outside services, sales, general and accounting costs, profits, etc. What they don't measure are the intangible costs associated with business such as the true costs of delay, defects, and deviations from standard or expected processes (the three D's)."* — Michele Nash-Hoff

Finding Help with TCO Calculation

Much of what I have described up to this point makes it difficult for companies to get assistance in developing accurate TCO calculations. Hypothetically, IT analyst firms should be good candidates for performing TCO analysis. Gartner, the largest IT analyst firm in the world, is actually credited with first introducing the concept of TCO to enterprise software. However, as has been discussed, most IT analyst firms have major conflicts of interest because they sell consulting services to vendors.[11] They also take considerably more money from the large vendors in comparison to the smaller vendors—and not coincidentally larger vendors tend to charge more for their software, more for their consulting, and so on. The upshot is that the TCOs of large vendors will be higher. Since the vast majority of IT analyst firms take the most money from vendors with the highest TCOs, they have little incentive to provide detailed TCO analyses, as doing so would probably cause them to lose some of their software vendor consulting revenues.

Also, different IT analyst firms have different interpretations of TCO. Gartner for instance tends to be "pro-TCO," while Forrester tends to be "anti-TCO," proposing that most companies cannot aspire to TCO successfully and that simpler approaches should be used. Forrester also points out that, according to their surveys, only about twenty-two percent of purchasing companies use any type of TCO in their decision-making.[12]

Is TCO Even Possible?
Several entities disagree on whether or not a full TCO analysis should be a goal. In this section we will review the concerns leveled frequently at TCO. One of the entities—which could be labeled as anti-TCO and which is influential in the area of enterprise software decision-making—is Forrester, the IT analyst firm.

"To really implement TCO-based analysis it takes a comprehensive and continuously updated catalog of asset inventory, in-service dates, agreed-upon operating cost rates for activities, and a scheme to divide shared costs among the constituent business processes that use them. For most firms, this is a pipe dream viewed either as a waste of resources in a futile quest for achievement or too intimidating to even begin. Forrester recommends a more expedient and realistic financial approach that can be just as effective but much simpler to calculate—relative cost of operations (RCO). RCO can be a middle-ground solution, moving far

---

[11] This topic is covered in detail in the SCM Focus Press book, *Gartner and the Magic Quadrant, a Guide for Buyers, Vendors and Investors.*

[12] http://www.forrester.com/TCO+Is+Overrated/fulltext/-/E-RES44545?docid=44545

beyond acquisition-cost-only analysis, while being more achievable than a full-blown TCO.” — Forrester

I agree with Forrester's assertion that companies rarely use TCO, but I do not see why performing a complete TCO analysis is beyond most companies if they are properly advised. We have performed a wide variety of TCO analyses for software categories and make these analyses available for a fee at our sub-site Software Decisions.[13] Because we take no money from vendors, we can legitimately say that our TCO analyses do not have a bias. One could always propose other non-financial biases—and these are possible and also come down to whether you consider exposure to a topic to be a bias or to be knowledge (babies after all are completely unbiased and open minded)—however, if one analyzes the major problem with respect to objectivity in analysis in not only the enterprise software arena, but also other areas such as financial advisement—consistently the problem is **financial** bias. This is true to such a degree that once financial bias is removed one has taken care of the vast majority of the problem. Forrester is not alone in their concerns regarding TCO.[14] The white paper *Rethinking TCO* takes a similar view of TCO as Forrester. *Rethinking TCO* points out some of the limitations of performing a meaningful TCO analysis when they state:

> *“The large amount of variability in product complexity and compre-hensiveness from one enterprise vendor is an important limitation on the potential for using TCO in multi-vendor analysis.”*

---

[13] Software Decisions can be found at http://www.softwaredecisions.org.

[14] Many people who use the term bias are not using it properly. Bias is not an opinion that disagrees with your own (common usage, by the way). Bias is a prejudice in favor of one thing or against another thing. The definition of a prejudice is a preconceived opinion that is not based upon reason or actual experience. (Google) Therefore bias is an invalid criticism of a judgment from experience, it is only a valid criticism of a pre-judgment, which is not based upon experience. A person with a contrary opinion—if it is derived from experience and if it is not influence by say a financial or relationship bias—is not biased. They simply have a contrary opinion.

However, this type of calculation will be performed either implicitly or explicitly (with an actual TCO); therefore, it is difficult to see how the approach of not performing the analysis is better than performing a TCO, especially considering what is at stake. In fact, merely performing the analysis—imperfect as it may be—puts a company in a more analytical frame of mind during their selection process.

Rethinking TCO also made the following argument against TCO.

> *"...different companies within the same industry may have significantly different business processes expressed in the same software product, or may have extensively customized a standard software package in order to gain some degree of competitive advantage. Indeed, this variability in use often represents a key strategic value for the enterprise software package: by using a standard software product in a nonstandard or customized fashion, many customers hope to gain competitive advantage over other companies in their industries that may be using the same or similar software."*

That is all true. However, this is where the implementation experience of individuals performing the TCO comes into play. If they are sufficiently experienced, they can increase or decrease the cost of a particular item through their knowledge of how much customization can be expected on the project. Furthermore, a non-customized TCO value probably would not make a lot of sense. It appears that this is an argument against non-customized TCO calculations.

> *"The implementation process is another major factor that adds to the problems with using TCO as a vendor selection tool. Implementation costs figure as one of the largest single expenses in enterprise software, and yet they are neither standardized nor consistent from one vendor to the next or one implementer, or implementation, to the next."*

While true, this can easily be accounted for in the TCO estimation, so it is difficult to understand the exact concern. Yes, implementation times can be adjusted for TCO estimations. And that is not the end of it; maintenance is quite different from one software vendor to the next and we adjust the maintenance costs per software vendor.

At Software Decisions, we account for all of these differences in the TCO estimation. For example, if an implementation is from a large consulting company, we adjust the estimate accordingly. If the implementation involves a large brand-name software vendor, we again extend the implementation timeline. For example, when we develop estimates for software vendors like SAP (which is neither designed to be easily implemented or easily used), we impose **higher costs** than any other software in the enterprise market. SAP takes longer to install, which means implementation costs are high, as are maintenance costs. This is why it is so important to check that the software functionality is reliable and usable; not only is the application more effective, the cost of the implementation is reduced, thus reducing its TCO and increasing its ROI. This goes back to a central theme of this book: without quantification through something like a TCO process, reliability and usability may be presumed to be equivalent between various software applications, when, in fact, they are quite different. Strangely, no one seems to bring up the issues that arise if costs that are assumed to be equivalent end up being quite different, making it difficult to make good decisions.

Conclusion

For the reasons listed in this chapter, consulting companies and purchasing companies spend a lot more time talking about TCO estimations than actually performing them. This is consistent with how purchasing and consulting companies present themselves: more rational than they actually are! Companies that implement enterprise software often skip TCO evaluations because they require effort and would get in the way of making trendy purchases. Most executive decision makers tend to believe in safety in numbers, and that means buying and implementing what other companies are buying and implementing. As for consulting companies, because they are surrogate software sales entities (that is, their interests are aligned with software sales because these sales drive consulting revenue), they are not oriented to the consumer or purchasing side. Neither are consulting sales entities, regardless of their ostensible position as "advisors." They are the sellers, so unless they take their advisement function seriously (which they don't) and were principled about this (which would mean sacrificing revenues for this principle), then consulting companies must be seen as lacking the objectivity to perform proper TCO analyses. The exception to this would be a smaller "boutique" consulting company or research company that is not involved in selling and in no way benefits from the purchasing decision.

CHAPTER 4

ERP: The Multi Billion Dollar TCO Analysis Failure

In the field of enterprise software, one of the most amazing stories of the past several decades is the mass purchasing of ERP systems—purchases made without the customers searching for evidence that ERP systems are good investments. If they had looked, they would have found that the logic presented to sell ERP systems had no evidence to support it. In the early phase of ERP's adoption, the excuse could have been made that the systems were new and studies had not yet been performed. However, thirty years after ERP systems were first adopted, that excuse no longer holds any water. This story is explained in detail in the SCM Focus Press book, *The Real Story Behind ERP: Separating Fact from Fiction*.

The adoption of ERP systems by so many companies occurred with very little actual research on the part of the parties involved either in making the purchases or in recommending the systems. The vast majority of ERP purchases were made without TCO calculations performed, which is why I dedicated a chapter of this book to ERP—it is such an amazing example of what happens when decisions are made without the necessary research—and instead of research large groups of individuals simply buy what other companies are buying—all the while assuming "someone else must have checked." This short chapter will illuminate what happens when purchasing decisions are made without sufficient research. These long-lived mistakes with respect to ERP have affected every part of IT today. ERP systems turned out to be vastly more expensive that even the highest "generalized" cost estimates of purchasing companies, even though eighty percent of the time these companies performed no real estimation. Now the ERP systems consume a very substantial portion of the overall IT budget, particularly for companies that purchased from the most expensive "big ERP" vendors. Other applications have been crowded out, and almost any of these other applications would have a higher ROI than ERP. As I will cover in Chapter 6: "Using TCO for Better Decision Making," a poor intuitive feel for implementation of project costs continues to drive poor decisions and extends routinely mediocre ERP functionality.

Did Logic and Analysis or Trendiness Drive ERP Procurement Decisions?

ERP was sold to companies on the basis of a number of arguments, which are outlined in the SCM Focus Press book, *The Real Story Behind ERP: Separating Fact from Fiction*, and then analyzed. However, it must also be recognized that many ERP purchasing decisions were made because companies felt they simply needed to have ERP, and these decisions were driven by fear—such as the Y2K fear that drove so many ERP implementations—or by a herd mentality.

> *"Slater (1999) discusses the breadth of such problems as he notes that 'companies buy multi-million-dollar software packages only to find out they don't work—or at least they don't work well—for one of their key business processes.' The reason, Slater suggests, is that ERP software is so hot, the flames fanned by consultants and the technical press cause companies to simply push forward without dealing with such key restrictions."* — Technology Monoculture

Measuring Success?

Another reason that success is often overestimated is that companies do not even know the applications well enough to know that they have failed. That is, they cannot properly measure the output of their system. While the users may know the system does not work as desired, the executive decision makers often do not. In my own field, I have written a number of articles that explain that often some of the most advanced software available is configured incorrectly to such a degree that there was no point in implementing the sophisticated software that was chosen.

http://www.scmfocus.com/supplyplanning/2011/07/09/what-is-your-supply-planning-optimizer-optimizing/

http://www.scmfocus.com/inventoryoptimizationmultiechelon/2011/05/how-costs-are-really-set-in-cost-optimization-implementations/

When I have brought the topic up of analyzing the actual quality of the system output with several of my clients, I have sometimes been told that no time was allocated to fix the system and that we must *"hit the deadlines,"* which is loosely translated into rolling out the flawed configuration to new regions. The information I provide is often suppressed and never reaches the ultimate decision makers. I have also been asked to suppress what I know about the problems with the configuration and to make it sound as if the application were correctly configured when discussing it with the users. Therefore, the top decision makers are in effect insulated from accurate information about how systems perform and instead told that everything is on track. Furthermore, information is not only suppressed by consulting companies (which, of course, is incredibly common), frequently, the company's own IT department withholds information from their own business, which explains the fact that even IT and the business cannot agree on striving for an effective software solution because of the differing incentives between IT and the business.[15]

So, when analyzing how and why companies do not perform TCO, the first assumption to dispense with is that those companies have **rational** decision processes or have effective channels for transmitting information to decision makers. I could speak at length on this topic and have many articles that explain this in a multitude of different areas. However, to those with work experience, I suspect that this is not exactly new news, so I will finish with this topic here.

The High TCO of ERP

ERP systems sold on the benefits of lower costs have actually proven to be very expensive, not only to implement but also to maintain. ERP systems have continued to become more expensive in terms of their direct cost because when companies give so many modules over to one vendor, they also give up a lot of negotiating leverage. The ERP vendors use this leverage in several ways. One way is to sell uncompetitive software in other areas in the same account. From a marketing perspective, ERP sales are the "wedge" that gets the company into the account. Once the wedge is in place, ERP is in the catbird seat in terms of selling more software into the account.

A second way ERP vendors use this leverage is to increase the cost of the yearly support contract. Generally the TCO of on-premises ERP systems is considered to be high. The implementation time is the longest of any enterprise software category. And the term "implementation time" is laden with assumptions. For

---

[15] A film that should be shown in all classes on management is, *Thirteen Days*. This film dramatizes the US side of the events leading up to and during the Cuban Missile Crisis. It shows the opposing agendas of the Kennedy Administration (and the disagreements within the administration) versus the Pentagon. Essentially the Pentagon was interested in an invasion of Cuba (likely starting a war with the USSR) over the placement of nuclear missiles in Cuba by the Soviets. The Kennedy Administration favored a blockade. However, the Pentagon withheld information from the Kennedy Administration and engaged in tactics designed to escalate the conflict. What the film effectively demonstrates is the myth of one "side" as a single decision-making entity, and explains it as simply a group of competing interests that arrive at a course of action through exhaustive negotiation. I would not make this recommendation except for having read the book, *Thirteen Days*, from which the film was adapted, and finding the film to be quite faithful to the book, except in the treatment of the role played by Kevin Costner, whose role was enlarged to provide a first-person narrative for the audience. The book itself is respected as an accurate account of the events. I would enjoy a second movie that shows the events from the Soviet perspective.

instance, according to IDC, fifteen percent of survey respondents re-implemented their ERP software. What was the implementation time on those projects, one may wonder. However, finding detailed TCO studies on ERP systems is not easy. For this reason, at Software Decisions, we created TCO estimates for all of the major ERP applications, and several of the open source ERP applications.[16]

The High Opportunity Cost of ERP

An area of ERP that is underemphasized or simply ignored altogether is the opportunity costs of ERP. The term "opportunity cost" is not used all that frequently on IT projects, so let's define the term first before we explain how it can best be leveraged in decision making:

> *"In microeconomic theory, the opportunity cost of a choice is the value of the best alternative forgone, in a situation in which a choice needs to be made between several mutually exclusive alternatives given limited resources. Assuming the best choice is made, it is the 'cost' incurred by not enjoying the benefit that would be had by taking the second best choice available."* — Wikipedia

Costs are often described in general parlance as the amount that we pay for things. However, economists look at costs quite a bit differently. Promoters of ERP tend to present any benefits of ERP without acknowledging that the time and effort spent on the ERP project could have gone into other initiatives. The comparison should be between the gains from those systems versus the gains from ERP systems. Let's take a simple example. Let's imagine that I have no car. I have a hard time getting around town because I lack transportation. In order to improve my condition, I buy a tractor. After a week, I report that I am able to get around town much more efficiently, and compared to walking, am now much more mobile. With this background, have I established that the tractor was the best possible alternative? Obviously I have not proved this. I could have purchased any number of cars, almost any of them with lower operating costs than a tractor. Tractors are great, but not a good choice for the purpose of traveling around town. Therefore, the question is not whether a tractor can improve mobility more than no other alternative device, but whether the purchase of the tractor improved my

---

[16] This site can be viewed at http://www.softwaredecisions.org.

condition compared to the other alternatives (these alternatives could be a car, public transit, bicycle, etc.).

Does my argument about the evidence for why a tractor is the best vehicle sound silly? Well it should, but it is no sillier, no less evidence-based, than the argument presented for why ERP has helped companies. Most fallacies in life—from fad diets to exercise machines seen on television to ineffective medical treatments— are essentially based upon anecdotal evidence with no supporting research. The comparison of something against nothing is one of the major ways in which individuals are led to false conclusions. The comparison can never be between "something" and "nothing," but must be between two "somethings." People who compare something to nothing are stacking the deck in favor of the "something" and are not promoting research or a logical and serious framework.[17] A certain exercise cannot be compared against no exercise at all, unless the intent of the study is to show the benefits of exercise versus inactivity. All tasks that are per- formed, all effort that is expended, all resources that are dispensed—everything can be expended and dispensed in a variety of ways. The normal objective is to find the one best way.

The direct costs of ERP systems have continued to rise because when companies give over so many modules to one vendor, they also give up a lot of negotiating power. The ERP vendors use their increased leverage in several ways. One way is to sell uncompetitive software in other areas in the same account. A second way is to increase the cost of the yearly support contract. Generally the TCO of

---

[17] This is also how so many "me-too" pharmaceuticals are approved—drugs that copy pre-existing drugs on the market (but with a slight twist to the molecule) are not compared against the pre-existing drugs that they copy. Instead the copied drug merely needs to beat the placebo. Therefore, the pharmaceutical companies are never asked to show a net benefit over existing drugs in order to receive a patent, which they would not be able to do because the two drugs are essentially the same drug. This is explained by Marcia Angela, M.D. *"Second, the pharmaceutical industry is not especially innovative. As hard as it is to believe, only a handful of truly important drugs have been brought to market in recent years, and they were mostly based on taxpayer-funded research at academic institutions, small biotechnology com- panies, or the National Institutes of Health (NIH). The great majority of 'new' drugs are not new at all but merely variations of older drugs already on the market. These are called 'me-too' drugs. The idea is to grab a share of an established, lucrative market by producing something very similar to a top-selling drug. For instance, we now have six statins (Mevacor, Lipitor, Zocor, Pravachol, Lescol, and the newest, Crestor) on the market to lower cholesterol, all variants of the first."*

on-premises ERP systems is considered to be high compared to other application categories.

Conclusion

If this chapter has been surprising to you, you are not alone. When I first began researching the material for this chapter, I was unaware that every one of the proposed logics for the purchase and implementation of ERP systems would prove to not only be wrong, but also spectacularly wrong. I was stunned that these amazing mental errors had not been reported in trade publications, as the lack of articles on these errors means that a multitude of actors have been misleading readers as to the benefits of ERP systems. I don't necessarily believe that there was a nefarious motivation on the part of all the people who have written about ERP vendors over the years. Certainly, vendors and software companies have been writing marketing literature and have zero interest in printing the truth. However, many journalists lack research skills and instead simply repeat what they hear about ERP. Getting at the truth is why it is so important to perform actual research when making software selections, and this is true not only of the individual applications within a software category, but of the software category itself. As an example, in the late 1990s many companies purchased marketplace services, a classification of services that was introduced with great fanfare by both software vendors and IT analysts, as the following articles discuss.

http://www.scmfocus.com/scmhistory/2010/07/how-analysts-got-everything-wrong-on-marketplaces/

However, there was very little evidence that this trendy category—marketplace services—would work out. In fact, the only one that did was Covisint, but it is really only a shadow of what it was projected to be. That is interesting, because I worked in a software company that promoted these "marketplaces," and at the time they were pitched as the future of business-to-business commerce. These days there is a new software category that has no benefit other than allowing forecasting departments to falsify their forecast accuracy. This software category is called demand sensing, and there are several articles on this trendy software category at SCM Focus.

http://www.scmfocus.com/demandplanning/category/demand-sensing/

Bottom line: before companies begin making determinations between various software vendors within a software category, the company should establish both the TCO and the actual benefits of the software category.

CHAPTER 5

The TCO Method Used by Software Decisions

The term "methodology" comes from the Latin word methodologia, which is a combination of methodus (a mode of proceeding, a way of teaching, or a road) and logia or logy (the study of). Therefore, a methodology is the study of a mode of proceeding. A methodology is not a method, and a great many people who prefer to use a more sophisticated word rather than the accurate word confuses these terms. For instance, in supply chain planning, optimization is a "method"; it is not a methodology. A study of the methods employed in supply planning would be a methodology. A methodology is a *"design process for carrying out research or the development of a procedure and is not in itself an instrument for doing those things."*

One of the criticisms from Alan MacCormak's 2003 study is that many TCO studies simply include too few cost categories, as he explains in the quotation below:

> *"The main area in which studies differ is with respect to the number and type of costs that are included in a TCO*

calculation. At one end of the spectrum are studies that consider only one or two 'direct' costs, focusing mainly on the up-front cost of the particular software platform that is being evaluated. At the other end are studies that use a much more sophisticated assessment, capturing not only the direct costs involved in purchasing and maintaining and supporting a particular platform, but also the 'indirect' costs associated with the use of the system, such as the cost of downtime. Importantly, the more comprehensive studies typically find that the cost of purchasing or leasing the software represents only a small proportion of the TCO for a software platform. This illustrates the danger of relying on studies that use only partial data on cost as the basis for making IT investment decisions... It is interesting to note that evaluations of TCO are not always conducted in a consistent manner even within the same firm."

TCO
TCO, or Total Cost of Ownership, is the overall output of the process, and simply sums the costs of the four main TCO categories:

1. *Software Costs:* Software associated costs, such as the cost to purchase licenses, or for SaaS delivered software their monthly/yearly charge.

2. *Hardware Costs:* Cost for hardware on which the software is installed.

3. *Implementation Costs:* Consulting resources, consulting travel, training.

4. *Maintenance Costs:* Fully loaded internal resources and vendor support.

The TCO Cost Categories
What follows is all of the individual cost categories that make up the final TCO.

Software/License Costs

The license cost is the initial purchase price from the vendor for an on-premises delivered solution, or the ongoing monthly or yearly software cost if the software is purchased as a SaaS-delivered application, often called a subscription. Here it is important to estimate the costs for the equivalent product between the different vendors. For instance, at the time of this book's publishing, the software vendor Salesforce offers five different pricing levels, ranging from $5 per month per user all the way up to $250 per month per user. These pricing levels represent very different applications, even though they are all "Salesforce."

It is important that the software license costs used from each vendor are consistent across the vendors that are compared. For example, the business requirements must be matched against each application to find the appropriate application expense level. Secondly, other vendors do not simply charge for their software either at different levels of use or by the number of users, but **through a combination of both**. For instance, one of the software vendors analyzed at Software Decisions has two different user types, as well as add-on modules. Therefore, the yearly license/subscription cost is a combination of these two types of users, along with the specific functionality to be activated. If a customer does not need multi-currency or project accounting, then the customer does not pay for it. This is another advantage of SaaS software vendors: they can price their application for just what the customer needs because they are able to control the functionality used by the customer.

Hardware Costs

Hardware itself is a small component of the overall cost of enterprise software. This was not always the case. In fact, at one time computer hardware was so expensive it was not bought outright but rather was leased. But the phenomenal improvement in computing technology in the last four decades has reduced the costs and increased hardware performance to a stark degree. In the SCM Focus Press book, *Inventory Optimization and Multi Echelon Planning,* the graphic on the following page was used to show this improvement:

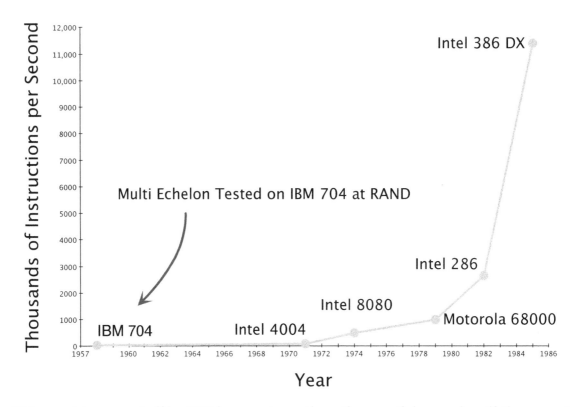

This graphic was cut off in 1986 because to continue the growth in speed until the present day would make the early increases imperceptible.

However, the hardware contribution to TCO cannot be restricted to the costs of the actual hardware. Other costs relevant for hardware include support: the cost of IT professionals to keep the hardware running, upgrading the hardware, fixing it, etc. Many individuals who specialize in hardware cost estimation use a factor of twenty percent to estimate the ongoing maintenance costs of hardware. However, the problem with this rule of thumb is that the maintenance costs for hardware are not proportional to the costs of the hardware. When more hardware than is strictly necessary for the predicted consumption of the application is purchased, this is called oversizing. When too little hardware has been purchased, this is referred to as undersizing. For instance, hardware that is oversized, and more expensive versus the need often requires **less care and feeding than hardware that is undersized**. Oversized hardware does not run into the constant limitations that under sizing requires. This entire topic is tricky because it intersects with the methods used in the software, the configuration of that software, as well as the timings of other related systems. For instance, while working with a previous client, I was shocked to find that the frequent problems we had experienced with processing time was because we were running the software on a **virtual server**. This means that the hardware was not dedicated to the software. Sometimes, when other applications were doing intensive processing, our processing times would be long because there was less of the processor to be allocated to our application. Undersized hardware not only increases the maintenance costs, but increases the software costs as well, as successive adjustments are made to things like processing times and batch schedules to make up for hardware limitations. And these two costs far exceed the costs of adding more hardware. The expense hierarchy basically is the following from highest to lowest.

1. Costs Incurred Through Software Adjustments

2. Costs Incurred Through Hardware Maintenance

3. Costs Incurred Through Adding Hardware

The process of sizing is the determination of the size of hardware, which must be purchased. It is quite common for companies to attempt to spend too much time sizing, and being concerned with making adjustments that reduce the size of the hardware and the money spent on hardware that end up costing more money in other ways. I have seen companies literally spend more money in performing hardware sizing than my client spent on the cost of the software itself. Spending a disproportionate amount on hardware sizing is easy to do if consultants are used to perform the hardware sizing (as their billing rate adds up quickly) or if the consultants' work is delayed because they are awaiting a decision on the hardware before they can move forward. Today, and likely in the future, the easiest answer to managing hardware limitations is to "throw hardware" at the problem.

When I discuss the types of errors made by IT, I am not talking about inexperienced IT departments from small companies. I am talking about IT departments with a lot of experience from the largest companies, and I am actually quite surprised by how few real hardware experts exist in IT departments who can size hardware across a variety of applications. One of the major issues is that IT departments are not experts in each application, and so there is a learning curve for each new application. As a result, software vendors are in the best position to perform hardware sizing as they have the greatest number of data points and, of course, developed the software. When SaaS software becomes more prevalent, one of the great benefits will be to take IT departments out of the business of buying and maintaining hardware. For instance, best-of-breed vendors such as Arena Solutions and Birst follow a multi-tenant model, where customers share one application but each customer uses a division of the database. The application is the same, but the data is not mixed up between the customers. Under the SaaS delivery model, hardware is far better utilized, as is explained by a quotation from the business intelligence software vendor Birst.

> *"This extremely variable computing load requires provisioning of greater computing power and generally results in lower hardware use than in conventional computing systems. It is not uncommon to have CPU and disk use at 1–4% in order to handle infrequent peaks of 60–80%. These low use levels result in particularly expensive hardware requirements. Cloud-based hardware virtualization does not address this as these systems must remain on and using CPU at all times, as user load is unpredictable. This is compounded if any degree of service level is required. To maintain uptime service levels, redundant hardware must be made available for clustering and failover, often doubling hardware infrastructure costs."*

SaaS software delivery has proven to be the most scalable and lowest cost approach to managing both hardware and software. Therefore, not only are software vendors in the best position to perform sizing, but under the SaaS and multi-tenant model, the vendor gets to spread its hardware over a large number of customers, meaning the hardware is more efficiently utilized. For instance, when Arena Solutions or Birst are asked to host a new customer, they are able to spread their hardware over many customers.[18] Software and hardware update decisions will

---

[18] Another benefit of SaaS vendors is when they introduce an upgrade/enhancement (which they first test in a separate environment), just as with Gmail, the customers "get" the update when they log into the system the next day. In most cases, the users have no idea that some improvement has occurred, although they can certainly check the online documentation to find out about the release notes, etc.

become invisible to the purchasing company, and it will be the job of the SaaS software vendor to simply maintain the performance outlined in the service level agreement with their customer.

Implementation Costs

Direct Estimation of Implementation Costs
Implementation costs are segmented into external costs and internal costs.

1. External implementation costs are the costs of consulting, which can come from the software vendor or from a consulting company.

2. Internal implementation costs are the costs that the company incurs during the implementation from using its internal resources. These are primarily the IT and business resources departments that are assigned to the project.

Both external and internal implementation costs can be determined several ways. Calculating various implementation durations along with the allocation percentage and the cost of each resource (the billable rate for external resources and the fully loaded costs for the internal resources) is the most accurate method of determining implementation cost **when one has first-hand experience implementing the software in question**.

However, as no one person has implemented all the software for which a TCO would be desired, it is necessary on many occasions to use multiple estimates. The most common multiple estimation is based upon the license cost. Therefore, if the cost of the software is $1,000,000 and the consulting to license cost multiple is two, the estimated consulting cost would be $2,000,000. Implementation multiples generally range from one to four. Some applications that are not implemented by large consulting companies from efficient software vendor's actually have a multiple that is less than one; however, true on-premises enterprise software will have a multiple higher than one. The only way to lower the multiple is to use SaaS solutions. At Software Decisions, the various TCO estimations—when they are multiple based rather than estimated from "the bottom up" change depending upon the application and the software vendor.

Multiple estimations from software vendors cannot be simply accepted, but must be blended with experience in implementation. Many software vendors quote a 1:1 ratio between software costs and consulting costs. However, this is not the extent of implementation costs. Software vendors only consider their consulting costs (although sometimes they add in training) and do not include internal resource costs for the implementing company. Generally, consultants from the software vendor provide the best consulting value. As soon as an outside consulting company is involved, the costs of the implementation go up. A major reason why SAP and Oracle implementations are so expensive compared to other implementations is these applications are typically implemented by the major consulting companies that have the highest implementation costs. As soon as a **major consulting company** is involved in the project, costs dramatically increase. The quid pro quo is very simple. The consulting company tells the software vendor *"we will recommend you, but only if you give us nearly all of the consulting business—if you don't do this we will not recommend you."* The consulting billings partially go to the consultants, but much of it is simply going to the management—that have very little to do with implementing the software. A partner at a large consulting company, out of the IT practice will make roughly $500,000 per year without ever touching the application being implemented. In addition to the partner's compensation, the major consulting companies also have large overhead in the form of offices (these often have to be prestigious in order to impress visiting clients), marketing (advertising and attending conferences), expense accounts, etc. Again, none of these things have **anything** to do with project work. At the end of the day, we estimate that roughly 1/3 of the billing rate, which is paid to the major consulting companies, actually goes to project work. But before we close the book on this topic, it's important to consider that the value is actually far worse than this. Aside from higher billing rates, major consulting companies tend to steer clients to the most expensive applications, and they also stretch out the length of the implementations, which of course greatly increases costs. In fact, it is because of the lack of involvement of large consulting companies in best-of-breed vendor implementations is another reason why best-of-breed solutions tend to score so much better in overall value, as is explained fully in the book, *Replacing Big ERP: Breaking the Big ERP Habit* *with Best of Breed Applications at a Fraction of the Cost.*[19] Therefore the implementation costs are entirely different if a major consulting company is involved. Therefore, to account for all of this, Software Decisions uses higher multiples if a client states that they are using a major consulting company, and companies performing TCO analysis themselves should do the same.

In the following paragraphs, we will review how to estimate implementation costs. This method is based on detailed first-hand knowledge.

External Implementation Costs

Sometimes implementation costs are best determined by using the following formula:

(Hourly Rate per Implementation Consultant × The Percent of Time Assigned to the Project × The Implementation Duration) + Travel Costs

Module Implementation Consultant

This is the hourly rate for the module implementation consultant, who is the more junior resource on the project from the consulting company or from the vendor.

The cost of this resource is calculated with the following formula:

(Hourly Rate × Percentage of Time on the Project) × Average of (Implementation Duration Low, Implementation Duration High) × 4.3 (weeks per year) × 40 (hrs)[20]

---

[19] Best of breed vendors typically cannot expect to be recommended by large consulting companies. In the cases where the best of breed vendor is selected, it is typically because the end client asked for them. However, even in this case, the ever resourceful consulting company will attempt to convince the best of breed vendor that "they" are bringing them in to the opportunity, and will squeeze concessions out of them (usually in the form of replacing some of the best of breed vendor's consultants with their own consultants who will need to learn on the client's time), or at least attempt to squeeze concessions out of them—even though the consulting company had no choice but to bring this software vendor in to the client.

[20] Consultants do take vacation, but they will often take vacation between projects, which is why the 4.3 weeks per month is assumed.

Senior Module Implementation Consultant

This is the hourly rate for the more senior module implementation consultant, who is the more senior resource on the project from the consulting company or from the vendor.

The cost of this resource is calculated using the following formula:

(Hourly Rate × Percentage of Time on the Project) × Average of (Implementation Duration Low, Implementation Duration High) × 4.3 (weeks per year) × 40 (hrs)

Senior Manager/Partner

This is the hourly rate for the more senior manager/partner, who is the most senior resource on the project from the consulting company or from the vendor. This resource will deal with project management issues, perform account management, acquire resources as needed, etc. These are not full-time resources, but tend to manage multiple projects (if they are from the vendor) or manage the overall program (of which the module being calculated here is just one part).

There is a separate line item for the percentage that each of these resources is on the project. Changing either the hourly rate or the percentage of time they are on the project adjusts the consulting costs. I won't list the explanations for the durations of each of the consulting line items, as they should be self-explanatory.

The cost of this resource is calculated with the following formula:

(Hourly Rate × Percentage of Time on the Project) × Average of (Implementation Duration Low, Implementation Duration High) × 4.3 (weeks per month) × 40 (hrs)

Travel Cost Assumption

This is for a project in the US. A project in Manhattan or San Francisco would be more expensive, and a project in Omaha, Nebraska would be less. Local resources, if a company can get them, would cost less—but of course it is not likely that the company would find local resources, and most often the local resources are not the best resources for the project. The travel cost is estimated at $45 per hour, and is then multiplied by the number of hours that the consultants are predicted to be on the project. This per hour estimate can be adjusted per the project's location. I developed the following expense estimate spreadsheet for a project in Seattle, for which I bid an all-inclusive rate (that is, I would pick up my expenses). Because I sometimes stay over weekends, I want to include both my cost of staying and the cost if I fly in and out of the city.

Travel Cost Estimation

	Hotel/Day	Flight/Week	Taxi to and from Airport	Meals/Day	Rental Car/Day	Weekly Expenses	Hourly Cost of Expenses
Stay Over The Weekend	$ 150.00			$ 45.00	$ 40.00		
Travel Friday to Monday		$ 500.00	$ 80.00				
Weekly Cost Stay Over	$ 1,050.00	$ -	$ -	$ 315.00	$ 280.00	$ 1,645.00	$ 41.13
Weekly Cost Travel	$ 750.00	$ 500.00	$ 80.00	$ 225.00	$ 200.00	$ 1,755.00	$ 43.88

As you can see, the estimates for staying over or flying out are about the same—just a few dollars more per hour for flying out. But, of course, the cost depends upon how far the flight is and how far in advance the flight is booked. Furthermore, the efficiency and on-site time of the consultant is lower if they fly in, as they do not appear at the client site until late Monday morning and have to leave by Friday (in some cases Thursday) in the early afternoon to catch their flight.

Internal Implementation Costs

The next area to estimate is the internal implementation costs.

Total Client Resource Costs for the Implementation

This is the total cost of staffing the client resources for the project. The formula we use for the total client resource costs is as follows:

The Total Client Resource Costs = (Implementation Duration in Weeks × The Opportunity Cost Per Week) × The Percent of the Average Week the Employee is assigned to the Project

The formula makes the following assumptions:

- The Implementation Duration in Weeks = (Average of the Duration in Months × 4.3)

- The Opportunity Cost Per Week = (The Number of Employees on the Project × The Hours Per Week × The Number of Weeks × The Fully Loaded Hourly Rate the Employee Costs the Company)

- The Percent of the Average Week the Employee is Assigned to the Project

The Percent Each Resource is Assigned to the Project

Most often, client resources assign part of their time to the project while retaining most of their other duties. The greater the number of applications included in the implementation, the more likely it is that internal resources will be one hundred percent allocated to the project. However, we are calculating the TCO for the implementation of one application only.

Implementation Duration

Implementation duration is measured from the beginning to the end of the implementation. The duration of a project cannot be predicted reliably to the month. Companies that attempt to meet deadlines that were predicted before the start of the project often end up with *faux* go-lives where the software is not really ready and they must continue to work intensively after the go-live date.

There are many factors that must be taken into consideration when estimating the implementation duration. Different clients have different levels of complexity and are in different areas of the application's functionality. Some clients may leverage older and more proven functionality, while others may choose to activate newer and less proven functionality. Some companies choose consulting companies that don't know the software very well, or can't document the solution.

Of all the many factors that go into the implementation duration, the most important *is the quality of the application itself, and specifically its implement-ability.* At SCM Focus we assign an implement-ability score to every application that we review. This is important, because so many companies simply assume—implicitly—that all software applications included in the software selection exercise are equally implementable. They don't differentiate based upon this factor. However, this is a false assumption. Some software is designed to be sold more than it is designed to be implemented. One of the best examples of this is SAP. At SAP, Sales has most of the say in the organization, and that the application "has" functionality is emphasized rather than making the functionality implementable. Therefore, SAP projects typically have many problems and take a long time to implement—and continue to have more problems after implementation. The best-of-breed applications that we compare to SAP are much easier to configure. More of the functionality works and the users find the application interface easier to use, so the implementation time is shorter. Companies that are unhappy with how long their implementations are taking, need to look at the software they are selecting because the application is the greatest determinant to both the project duration and the success of the implementation. We are really starting to see this happen in the business intelligence market, where the overwhelming cost and implementation time of self service applications like Tableau are making the TCO advantage almost too obvious to ignore versus older solutions in the market.

Realistic Project Implementation Duration Estimates
Most vendors would not be happy with the implementation duration estimates developed by Software Decisions. However, these estimates are based upon years of analyzing how applications are actually implemented, which is far from the optimum values that are often quoted. We have performed the research, and the

statistics are clearly on our side—enterprise software implementations take much longer than is generally assumed, not only by the software vendor, but also by the project management of the implementing company. There have been many attempts over the years to reduce implementation timelines, yet they remain sticky. One exception to this is SaaS, which consistently has shorter implementation durations than on-premises applications. SaaS delivered applications allow a company to get closer to the optimum implementation time. One reason for this is there are fewer hiccups and the infrastructure is already in place. In addition, more of the vendor's expertise can be leveraged at any time (the SaaS vendor has one hundred percent access to the application at any time because they control the box)—and that can mean literally **any time**; some SaaS vendors offer twenty-four hour support and since so many SaaS vendors offer some support from countries on opposite time zones—notably India—work can be done when clients are asleep in the US or Europe.

These are just a few factors that explain why SaaS implementations tend to be so much faster and smoother than implementations of on-premises applications. But most applications are not delivered through SaaS; they are delivered on-premises, and realistic implementation times are necessary because we are not developing TCO estimates for a perfect world, but for companies that have to implement software in this world.

Nucleus Research addresses this exact issue with other similar applications like i2 Technologies.

> *"Nearly 70 percent of the i2 deployments lasted longer than project teams had planned. For these companies, deployment took, on average, nearly three times longer than expected while increasing consulting personnel costs and slowing the realization of benefits from the solution.*

> *"Don't let vendors dictate your expectations of how long it will take to deploy a certain tool in your environment. Make an independent estimation based on internal planning and the experiences of similar companies that have implemented (the application)."*

Another factor that can lessen an application's overall implementation duration is that often people will not consider the durations of problematic implementations, as if for some reason problematic implementations don't count. It is unscientific to remove problematic implementations from the equation unless there is a very good reason to do so (such as the company stopping the implementation to work on a different project before returning to the implementation of the first application). This is called "outlier removal," and is a primary method by which research is falsified across disciplines, as discussed in the following article:

http://www.scmfocus.com/demandplanning/2010/07/outlier-removal/

I was recently contacted about a re-implementation project. For two years the company had attempted to implement a combination of SAP modules and never brought the system to a live state. It then waited a year and a half, and then attempted a re-implementation. What is the duration on this project?

There are other examples of problems in time estimation. Often an application will go live, but the company finds the application is not adding value to the business. I have seen this numerous times with applications where the configuration and settings were not set up in such a way that the business could benefit. Instead of adjusting the settings, which would have been the right thing to do, the faulty configuration was simply rolled out to more regions in order to keep on target with the initial timelines. A person in management may measure the time the application officially went live as its implementation time; however, the way this is measured at Software Decisions is that the application should not be counted as live until it begins to add value to the business. It is, in fact, quite easy to bring up an application so that it is "live." All that has to be done is client specific master data setup, integration performed to other systems and a generic configuration used. I refer to this as a **100% IT implementation**—the system is working and all the server lights are blinking. Implementing the software in a way that adds significant value is the actual goal not simply hitting a deadline. However, in multiple studies it has been found that companies have no other way of objectively determining project success beyond the meeting of project deadlines.

The Cost Implications of Implementation Duration

Implementation duration affects TCO in several important ways. The longer the project's duration, the more the expenses of the implementation add up because the consultants are on the project longer, and the longer it is until the company can begin seeing a payback from its efforts (however, this is an ROI issue not a TCO issue).

Multiple-based Estimation of Implementation Costs

The second way of estimating implementation costs is by using a multiple of the software/subscription cost. It's an easy way of estimating the implementation costs because the external or internal costs are not estimated separately. However, which multiple is chosen is, of course, of primary importance. If this information is not determined from projects, it must be triangulated from multiple independent sources, and of course, finding independent sources that will share this type of information is tricky. Software Decisions conducts interviews with a number of individuals with expertise, but people generally do not like going on the record when they report their implementation experiences.

Various TCO Implementation Estimates Versus Software Decisions Estimates

In one example, the study *What Managers Should Know About ERP/ERP II* estimates ERP software license costs to be between ten and twenty percent of the overall TCO. That is significantly higher than the estimates at Software Decisions for ERP software, which show that the average cost across multiple software categories is approximately ten percent. We think this is because our TCO model is more comprehensive, and therefore, we have a higher "TCO" than the "TCO" produced by other entities. The book, *Control Your ERP Destiny: Reduce Project Costs, Mitigate Risks, and Design Better Business Solutions* considers a reasonable estimate of the ERP software costs to be twenty percent of the total project budget, but states that software vendors tell their potential customers (as do consulting companies) that **consulting costs will be roughly twice the cost of the software**. However, these are only the external implementation costs and not the internal implementation costs.

It seems strange that so many sources limit implementation costs to the consulting costs, when it is well recognized that internal team members must always be assigned to enterprise software implementation projects for some percentage of their weekly hours. Sometimes internal resources are pulled off their normal duties entirely and one hundred percent of their time is assigned to the implementation project—this is very common on ERP implementations. However, on many other types of enterprise software implementations, internal resources share duties. One independent source, 180systems, actually estimates that consulting costs average sixty-five percent of the license costs (seventy-one percent for larger customers and fifty-nine percent for mid-sized customers).[21, 22]

A meta-analysis and comparison of my individual TCO analyses is provided below.

Cost Estimates and Comparison from Four Application TCO Analysis

Costs	Supply Planning	Production Planning	Demand Planning	Service Parts Planning	**Average**
Software Costs	11.0%	16.0%	9%	14%	**12.5%**
Consulting Costs	27.0%	19.0%	28%	25%	**24.8%**
Consulting Costs Divided by Software Costs	245%	119%	311%	179%	**213.5%**
Percentage of Total Six Year Costs	38.0%	35.0%	37.0%	39.0%	**37.3%**

The software vendors' estimate of consulting costs being roughly twice the software cost holds true for my sample (although you can see also that there is considerable variability). However, this does not correlate with our estimations **because other TCO estimations that we have reviewed consistently underestimate the TCO of applications.** *License costs are explicit costs and therefore the easiest to estimate, but they are also the easiest to overestimate in relation to other costs.*

One source that does check out is E2BEnterprise. They provide an estimate, which is consistent with the independent estimation produced by Software Decisions.

---

[21] http://www.camagazine.com/archives/print-edition/2011/aug/columns/camagazine50480.aspx.

[22] Estimations from other sources are all over the map. Some entities recommend a rule of thumb of 1:1 between license and consulting costs.

E2BEnterprise recommends a ratio of anywhere from 1:3 to 1:4 between software and consulting costs for ERP implementations. According to James Mallory of E2BEnterprise, SMB ERP implementations can be as low as 1:1 or 1:2 but only to implement the bare minimum core system. This is common for companies that have a short window for implementation or tight budgets. But costs for a streamlined implementation provide for streamlined capabilities. Companies must continue to implement new modules and other areas of the system in order to gain significant efficiencies and the end result for a proper implementation will result in a total investment closer to 1:3 or 1:4 in the end—it just depends on when you make that investment—up-front or over the course of several years.

Here are some important aspects to consider when evaluating TCO studies:

1. The implementation expenditures for some software categories (for instance, ERP implementation projects) are **consistently and significantly over-budget; however, ERP software vendors simply do not include going over-budget in their TCO estimates or, of course, in their project timelines.** If the project goes over-budget, no estimate provided by a software vendor applies.

2. What is the TCO for software that is never implemented or severely delayed? This is a confusing question to answer. I have interviewed for several projects that were re-implementations, and have worked on a few. A re-implementation may occur if the software failed to go live—that failure may have taken place over the course of a year and a half. The company focuses on other things, and then two and a half years after it began the first implementation, decides to re-implement the software. If the software is taken live the second time, this project will most likely have a negative ROI. **No software vendor or implementing company** wants to talk about these types of projects, but the historical (not hypothetical) implementation timelines must be incorporated into future projections. Anything less than this and the TCO calculation is being fudged to meet a predetermined outcome. If, depending upon the study used, between fifty percent (Barker and Frolick) and ninety percent (Scott and Vessey) of ERP implementations fail, and if the vast majority of ERP implementations miss their deadlines

by significant durations, why are TCO estimates still based upon assumptions that do not include these very critical factors?

3. Depending upon the study used, between eighty-seven percent and ninety-six percent of ERP implementations include moderate to extensive customizations. Customization results in high implementation costs, high continuous improvement costs, and high maintenance costs. Other software categories have various degrees of customization—almost always less than ERP—so ERP should receive the highest bump for coding-related implementation costs.

Training Costs

Training costs fall into several categories. Most software vendors either send the training out to the implementing company (if there is a sufficient number of company resources in the class), or the implementing company sends its resources to the software vendor's training facility. But this is not the end of the training costs. The salary costs of the people being trained must be included, as these people are not able to do their regular work during the training.

The formula that we use for this standard training model is the following.

Total Training Costs = The Training Cost Per Week + The Opportunity Cost Per Week

- The Training Cost Per Week = (Number of Employees Sent to Training × Vendor Charge Per Employee Per Week × The Number of Weeks)

- The Opportunity Cost Per Week = (The Number of Employees Sent to Training × The Hours Per Week × The Number of Weeks × The Fully Loaded Hourly Rate the Employee Costs the Company)

Not all resources from the implementing company spend the same amount of time in training. Some resources are assigned to become resources, which mean they take on some of the internal training and long-term support for the application. These "super user" resources must be estimated at a higher level than normal users.

Integration Costs

Integration costs are simply included in the overall implementation costs because breaking out the integration effort is unnecessarily complicated—it is far simpler to estimate the overall implementation costs. Furthermore, many companies— SAP and Oracle come to mind—lead executives to believe that they will incur minimal integration overhead if they purchase one of their non-ERP applications to connect to the implementing company's ERP applications; this is untrue. All of SAP and Oracle's applications sit on different hardware, and while they may have adapters, they are not actually integrated—they have different databases. (The term "integrated" is used colloquially to mean any connected systems, but most accurately it means that the systems use the same database. When systems have adapters between them, they are not technically integrated.) Often the quality and ease-of-use of these adapters is inferior to the adapters that are written to connect best-of-breed applications to the ERP system.

Maintenance Costs

Maintenance costs are the costs of keeping the application up and running after the go-live, and are some of the most underestimated enterprise software costs. These costs are comprised of both the yearly support fee as well as the internal labor costs of providing support.

Internal Maintenance Costs

Internal maintenance costs represent the allocation of internal resources to maintaining the application for its lifetime in the company, and are calculated with the following formula.

Internal Maintenance Cost = The Fully Loaded Resource Cost Per Year × The Average Allocation of Time to Support the Application × The Number of Years the Application is Used

The number of years an application is used is an estimate based upon the software category. Different software categories have different average durations of use in companies. This is addressed shortly.

Vendor Yearly Support Costs

The vendor's yearly support costs change depending upon whether the software is delivered as on-premises or SaaS. Support fees tended to be lower in the past, but as software vendors learned that companies overemphasize their software purchase price versus other costs and have no idea how to perform TCO estimations, the vendors reduced the up-front costs and have increased their support costs. For example, vendors have reduced their initial license fee and increased their support fees. Large ERP vendors have set twenty percent as the standard service fee, but depending upon the vendor, a reduced rate can sometimes be negotiated for this service fee. With SaaS-delivered applications, the service fee is bundled into the yearly subscription so there is no separate fee to calculate. Overall, this is one of the easier numbers to obtain from software vendors.

Total Years the Application Is Used By the Company

How many years the company will use the application is difficult to estimate. The following quotation, which was obtained from interviews on this topic (this source prefers to be anonymous), explains why:

> *"If the software works well—meaning good configuration and good training, along with a group of super users—an advanced planning application can be kept in use for seven to ten years. However, if a new CIO comes by, an application's life can be only three to five years."*

There is really no perfect way to estimate this value, and it is difficult to know how long the application will be in use in the company. Furthermore, an application that does not work very well can be kept too long—often for political reasons—while an application that is working well can be replaced due to issues that are related to what happens to be popular at the time. This was known to be true of i2 Technologies (a supply chain planning vendor), which often had software that was installed and working well at some accounts that we reviewed. However, SAP's products had become more popular, and so the i2 Technologies products that were functioning fine were removed and the SAP products were implemented, often without improving the condition of the company.[23] This decision to replace i2 Technologies' applications was driven partly by trendiness and partly by concerns about the financial strength of i2 Technologies.

Not understanding the limitations of the implemented application is another cause of unnecessary turnover to a new application. After implementing an application, the implementing company becomes familiar with all of the application's limitations. The marketing hyperbole in another software vendor's literature starts to sound quite appealing. Furthermore, often apples are being compared to oranges. At one of my clients there was dissatisfaction with the current system; however, the system had not been upgraded for roughly thirteen years. Compared to the new system we were installing, it had an old user interface and was dated in some ways. Rather than installing an application, a better choice would have been to simply pay to upgrade the current system, because after several months working with me and seeing all the limitations of the new system, one of the business leads said *"can we go back to the old system?"* This was said only partially in jest, because the new system was going to set the company back in a number of ways, and it was difficult for me to see how the company was even going to be able to get a payback from the software that I was helping them implement. The older software was a better fit for their needs and they had already been trained on how to use it. Once again, the executives for this company had no idea what they actually bought, but instead had been persuaded to buy the new application on the basis of hype and one particular vendor being "hot" in the market.

At Software Decisions the estimates for an application's life expectancy are adjusted per software category. Our standard estimate is seven years, but we may go longer or shorter depending upon the application type. In some cases we will go with five years or even three years. Because of this variability, the TCO estimate should be given as an average per year (and also an average per year per user) in order to normalize the TCOs between applications in various categories. On the other hand, ERP systems tend to be longer-lived, averaging

---

[23] Enterprise software is surprisingly like the fashion industry in that regard. A software vendor will get "hot" and then everyone feels like they have to have it. Part of this is also a signal from the company to Wall Street; companies will buy software that they think Wall Street will look upon favorably, even though neither the purchasing company nor the Wall Street analyst who is grading the stock may have used the software.

between eight and twelve years. ERP systems take so long to implement that it's infeasible to replace them more frequently. On-premises applications tend to have longer lifespans because they are more difficult to re-implement; that is, they have more lock-in. SaaS offers the potential of being able to switch between software vendors much more quickly. Because they have less invested, SaaS applications have less lock-in than on-premises applications. Generally speaking, the ability to switch vendors easily would be a tremendous benefit to enterprise software because—as has been pointed out repeatedly—many companies frequently make poorly informed software selection decisions and are therefore stuck with a bad application for years. This is, of course, why Excel and Access use is so high in many companies. Excel is used as the patch—the ultimate backup—when the purchased application cannot meet the business requirements.

Number of Support Resources Required for the Life of an Application

Support resources include everyone required to support the application: technical, functional and management. It should never be assumed that the support "load" on internal resources **is equivalent, even between applications in the same software category**. There is a marked difference between vendors—and the degree to which the applications have been designed to be maintainable. This maintainability can be everything from how easy the application is to use (its usability: more usable applications require less hand-holding to accomplish tasks) to how straightforward it is to update its master data.

Internal Support Costs and Outsourcing

When reviewing Software Decisions TCO analyses, software vendors will typically respond that the internal support amount should be lower. Often they only estimate their own support costs, and when they do acknowledge the internal support costs, they will only estimate **the internal IT resources** required to support their application. While that approach was never accurate, it is even less accurate now because companies are responsible for more "self-support" today than ever before. And this is, in part, due to the IT outsourcing trend. Outsourcing makes CIOs look great from the perspective of costs. However, in the vast majority of cases we have reviewed, outsourced IT support means a reduced IT support level. Applications are utilized at a lower level and problems take longer to fix. The major consulting companies produce most articles on this topic; as they have significant outsourcing businesses themselves, the information they provide is unreliable.[24] Furthermore, none of the major consulting companies have demonstrated that they are competent at performing IT support versus selling IT support. At client after client I have worked with the outsourced support is mismanaged and the business unhappy with the support that they receive.[25] Essentially outsourcing has made IT less efficient and while outsourcing may have resulted in fewer IT resources within companies, it has also meant negative externalities in the form of lower support that must be performed by the business. Therefore, the lowered costs (although at very high margins with little money paid to the workers providing the support—mostly in India) have not been able to maintain quality levels. It is possible to imagine high-quality outsourcing, but while that may exist hypothetically, the reality of outsourcing is a movement to reducing costs while ignoring reduced quality. Therefore, the total cost of supporting applications is far greater than simply the costs of IT resources assigned to support the application.

Analyzing Project Risk

Up until this point we have left out the discussion of risk adjustment. However, **every TCO analysis** also has a risk associated with it. This is important because while one application may score better in functionality, it may be far riskier in that the implementation has a lower likelihood of success. Without risk estimation, by default all applications will be graded equally on risk, which penalizes the lower-risk applications. In fact, some of the riskiest applications that I have analyzed are some of the most popular. Like a risky 401k investment that is

---

[24] Some journalists will state that the main issue is offshoring—that is outsourcing to low cost countries—but that outsourcing is viable. In fact, if we look at SaaS, this is "outsourcing" much of the IT support for an application—although it is of a different nature as the software vendor has a comparative advantage in their own application and they host and control it. However, as practiced, outsourcing refers to a large consulting company offering resources from countries with very low wages. The consulting company then bills out these resources at a much higher rate than they pay them. This is the predominant method of outsourcing, and this is what I am referring to in this section.

[25] There seems to be a great number of apologists for outsourcing in the IT press. All the major consulting companies are advertisers in these outlets, and they will interview their advertisers on various issues to determine the editorial approach they should take. Articles that don't gel with advertisers don't get covered. The evidence on the advertising's impact on media content is very well established, and is from multiple sources. One of the best known research being the investigation into the coverage of the health issues of tobacco with media outlets that took advertising money from cigarette companies. Those media outlets that took cigarette advertising did not report information on tobacco's connection to cancer. Advertising's influence on the media output in **enterprise software** is covered in the SCM Focus Press book, *Gartner and the Magic Quadrant: A Guide for Buyers, Vendors, Investors.*

pushed by a paid off financial advisor, enterprise software buyers often have no idea how risky the software they buy actually is. A great reason for this is that applications are simply not risk analyzed before purchase. Given the high failure rate of enterprise software implementations, it makes sense to include risk in all decision making. The Software Decisions risk factor is **a composite value that is made up of multiple factors**, some associated with the application, some with the specific functionality to be implemented, and some with the implementing partner. I will not delve further into risk here; for more on the topic, please refer to the SCM Focus Press book, *Enterprise Software Risk: Controlling the Main Risk Factors on IT Projects*.

CHAPTER 6

Using TCO for Better Decision Making

Developing the TCO estimations is the difficult part. The more interesting part is actually using the TCO, as there many varied uses. TCO can be used specifically or generally. For instance, once one has a handle on TCO for an application area, the TCO can be used to make future decisions after the purchase has been made. This is best explained with an example, and one came up while I was writing this book.

Example: TCO and Continuous Improvement
I was developing a proposal for an audit of an application that was already installed and live. This audit was designed to offer areas of improvement in the application. To provide some context, the following text was used on one of the slides from my proposal presentation:

> *"In software implementation, much of the focus is on the initial acquisition and the implementation. However, the measurement of optimal usage and received benefits can be a tricky proposition. To do this requires seeing the application in a variety of environments, and comparing the configuration and planning the outcomes. The audit provides*

important feedback toward the software implementation's current usage and potential areas of improvement.

1. *Some functionality may not be working exactly as desired.*

2. *An unknown feeling as to how much and/or well the investment in the application is being leveraged.*

3. *Issues with, or concerns that, the application may not be optimally integrated (both technically and process–wise) to the other applications in the company."*

Many companies are interested in such an audit if produced by an objective source. However, the question of the price eventually comes up, and while a consulting rate can be fiddled with, the biggest issue is the duration of the audit project. Previous audits/evaluations I had performed typically ranged from one week to three weeks. However, those who wanted a shorter audit based their logic upon the idea that the cost would be too high, as the audit would cost between $12,832 and $14,560. There was no way that some of the companies that had spent roughly $100,000 for both the software and the implementation (this was inexpensive enterprise software) would be willing to spend what could be close to $15,000 for an audit—or what amounted to **fifteen percent** of the total cost of the software and implementation.

However, the problem with this way of thinking is that the cost of the software license and implementation is **not the company's TCO** for the life of the application and therefore should not serve as the estimation of its investment. The TCO studies at Software Decisions show that the software and implementation costs for the application in question represented only about thirty percent of the application's TCO. Other costs included hardware and maintenance. We can estimate the TCO for customers who spent $100,000 for just the software and implementation (consulting), and this is done in the following spreadsheet.

Audit Project Estimate

Consulting Costs

Rate Assumption 1			*Rate Assumption 2*		
Hourly Rate	$	180	Hourly Rate	$	156
Hour Estimate			Hour Estimate		
Straight Time	$	68	Straight Time	$	68
Part Time	$	4	Part Time	$	4
Billing	$	12,960	Billing	$	11,232
Travel Cost	$	1,600	Travel Cost	$	1,600
Total Cost	$	14,560	Total Cost	$	12,832
Typical PT Customer's Overall Expenditure (License & Consulting)	$	100,000		$	100,000

*Based upon Software Decisions analysis of this application. Audit should be justified on the percentage of their overall expenditure for the application.

Other Costs	$	333,333		$	333,333
Total/TCO	$	433,333		$	433,333
Audit as Percentage of Overall Total Cost of Ownership		3.4%			3.0%

From this analysis, it does not seem as if the company should be so concerned about the audit's cost. The cost of an audit is not fifteen percent of the customer's cost, but would be between 3% and 3.4% of the application's TCO.

This is a far more logical context within which to make a decision about seeking advice about a solution. Of course, this says nothing about the quality of the audit; this TCO analysis simply provides a context within which to perform the cost-benefit analysis. The audit can provide good results or bad results depending upon the knowledge level and incentives of the individuals performing the audit.

After TCO is developed, it can be put to use in supporting decision-making in a variety of ways, as shown in the example above. Companies should really have TCO analyses performed for all of their applications. It is quite common for companies to make decisions to extend use of their ERP system in some area, usually functionality that is known to be mediocre; however, the decision is driven by the desire to *"get more value from our ERP system"* or to *"leverage our ERP invest-ment."* These can seem like desirable goals, until one begins to look through the lens of TCO. When executives state that they want to leverage ERP by utilizing more of that ERP system's functionality, exactly what is being leveraged should be understood. In fact, the only thing that is being leveraged is the software license fee, possibly some hardware cost and support fee—but not the implementation costs, some of the hardware cost, and not overall maintenance cost.[26] However, if the hardware cost is taken at a fifty percent value (which either way is a minor portion of the TCO), then the average costs for the license fee, hardware costs, and the support fee across a wide variety of applications come to roughly **fifteen percent** of the TCO of any new application implementation. And this means not using an application, which would win in a software selection, rather this is simply using the application that happens to be "around."

Overall, *"leveraging"* any current software, be it ERP or other software that the company owns, will not typically save the company more than fifteen percent of the TCO of the functionality in that area. Depending upon the situation, there can be more integration costs.[27] However, while the company saves roughly fifteen percent on the TCO of the new functionality/application, making this decision will, in most cases, greatly reduce the ROI of the initiative.

Reducing ROI Through Lowered Functionality
How easy is it to reduce the ROI on a software project by at least fifteen percent? By using software that is not particularly adept in an area compared to competing options, not only is it easy—it is almost assured. According to statistics that are commonly quoted, software implementations have a success rate of roughly fifty percent depending upon how the question in the survey is asked. By our estimates,

---

[26] The support fee paid to the vendor on a yearly basis is only one small component of the maintenance costs.

[27] This greatly depends upon what the integration is with the present solution. Applications from the same vendor are often much less integrated than appears in the sales presentation. Furthermore, most best-of-breed vendors have quite a bit of experience, and often adapters that can connect to, particularly, the more popular ERP systems. But pre-written adapters from both ERP companies and best-of-breed vendors are uniformly overestimated in sales presentations versus their actual on-project performance. If you are interested in an example of a detailed explanation of how much a pre-written adapter can differ from what is presented in the sales process, see this article. http://www.scmfocus.com/sapplanning/2011/05/19/why-i-no-longer-recommend-using-the-cif/.

this is too high, for several good reasons. Some companies that deem the solution to be a success do not know the software area well enough to know how little the application offers over previous approaches to solving the same problem. Off the top of my head I can recall a number of projects where the application does very little to improve on the previous solution, but that truth is hidden from the client by the consulting company or by their own IT department. The business users know, but the executives—who mostly fill out the success/failure question-naires—would not know.

So, trying to save fifteen percent on the cost of the implementation with absolutely no consideration for the potential ROI (which is the dominant approach to soft-ware selection and decision making in US companies) is one of many factors that keep the success rate of IT implementations so low, and probably lower than the commonly quoted statistics would lead one to believe. In fact, with IT implementa-tions as risky as they are, the **implementing company needs every possible advantage it can get, and trying to save fifteen percent in what is just one category of costs is not the way to do it**. Choosing the best application for the job is the first step in increasing the likelihood of a project's success.

The End Result of Not Using TCO to Inform Decision Making
Deciding to leverage what is *"already purchased"* (a misleading term as it should be rephrased as leveraging what is *"already fifteen percent purchased"*) will most often mean taking a **major hit in functionality** and in the ability of the users to perform the activities in the system that the company is asking them to perform. Furthermore, this line of thinking assumes that all other costs—that is the other eighty-five percent of costs—are roughly equivalent. However, they are anything but equivalent. On a direct functionality-to-functionality basis, ERP systems are the most expensive systems to implement and to maintain. This is demonstrated by the TCO studies at Software Decisions. ERP systems are almost always combined with **customization,** estimates range from 87 to 93% of ERP implementations have from moderate to extensive customization. This customization lengthens out the implementation timeline, which results in increased implementation costs and higher long-term maintenance costs.[28] This is a primary reason why so many

---

[28] Estimations and sources related to the customization burden of ERP systems can be found in *The Real Story Behind ERP: Separating Fact from Fiction.*

companies have continued to implement uncompetitive functionality in their ERP systems when so many better solutions were available in the marketplace, they are attempting to utilize their pre-existing investment in their ERP system. However, research at our companion site Software Decisions demonstrates that this is a faulty logic as companies can only expect to save 12.5% of the application's TCO by leveraging the sunk cost of a previously implemented ERP system. [29] Other applications that are specifically designed to meet business requirements (aka best of breed) have better ratings in a variety of compensating criteria. Because of this, it is a simple matter to exceed this cost savings with an increased likelihood of the following:

1. A Longer Implementation

2. More Customization Expense

3. A Higher Risk Implementation

4. Lower Functionality/Worse Fit of Functionality

5. Lower Usability

6. Lower Maintainability

---

[29] This website can be viewed at http://www.softwaredecisions.org.

CHAPTER 7

Combining TCO Analyses for a Complete Enterprise Solution Architecture

TCO presents an opportunity far greater than that presented by its general interpretation. TCO is often discussed in terms of its value for doing things such as assisting with the decision regarding a specific application. As such, many people—and this is true even of proponents of TCO—often frame the benefits of TCO far too narrowly. In fact, there is no reason to limit the use of TCO because TCO can assist in selecting the ***overall enterprise software strategy for a company***. That is, TCO can be used to compare multiple applications to make decisions between different software categories.

In Chapter 4: "ERP: Multi Billion Dollar TCO Analysis Failure," it explains how the cognitive errors that allowed ERP to flourish were due to a lack of overall analysis and to the "advice" that was provided by biased parties, including advice from those who accepted direct payments from ERP vendors and guidance from consulting companies that make enormous sums of money from ERP implementations. The review of the research, which is explained in the SCM Focus Press book, *The Real Story Behind ERP: Separating Fact from Fiction,* demonstrates that none of the projections for ERP came true. These projections were always based upon a feeble logical foundation, and although the logic used to sell ERP was based upon rosy projections, the vast majority of companies lacked the internal research capabilities to validate these claims.

One type of analysis that was not done (and more shockingly, was not done even decades after the research became apparent on ERP) was TCO analysis. Most companies bought ERP systems on a combination of blind faith and the need to signal to a variety of parties (the stock market, suppliers, B2B customers, etc.) that they were making intelligent and forward looking decisions.[30] After we reviewed all of the research on the topic, it became clear that ERP did not improve the operations or the financial performance of companies. As a result we decided to add several TCO estimators to the Software Decisions website. One of these estimators compared a non-ERP solution to a one-hundred-percent best-of-breed solution. In order to build this estimator, we:

1. Estimate the TCO for each of the individual best-of-breed applications.

2. Estimate the TCO for a one-hundred-percent ERP vendor solution. This would include the ERP system combined with the ERP vendor applications outside of ERP (business intelligence, advanced planning, CRM, etc.).

3. Estimate the functionality, implement-ability, usability and maintainability differential between the best-of-breed master solution (the one-hundred-percent best-of-breed solution) and the one-hundred-percent ERP vendor solution.

---

[30] Although it should be noted that this motivation also did not result in benefits, as the research clearly demonstrates that ERP systems do not improve the financial performance of the companies that implement them, nor do they improve the stock price—either through improved operations or through signaling to investors—in any shape or form.

In addition to this comparison, we added another TCO estimation that compares a one-hundred-percent best-of-breed solution from a Tier 1 vendor to a combination of a Tier 2 ERP vendor with best-of-breed applications connected to it. This would give us three points of comparison. Once we estimated TCO for these three points of comparison, along with application estimations in the areas of functionality, implement-ability, usability and maintainability, we would be in an excellent position to provide the highest level of advice on solution strategy to companies.

The Combined Enterprise Evaluation Method

To accomplish the above, it was necessary to find and calculate the TCO for multiple software categories—in fact for most of the commonly implemented software categories. There are, of course, several challenges to doing so. First, we had to adjust the Software Decisions TCO method for different types of cost drivers. Software vendors have many different categories of costs, and not all software vendors use the same categories. Therefore normalizing of TCO estimations across many different software vendors is necessary. Normalization is necessary across many of the cost categories, and giving any one vendor a cost advantage **can tilt the decision-making in their favor**. For example, even within one software category, implementation times can vary greatly. The average estimated implementation time must be reflected in the TCO estimations for vendors with applications that are difficult to implement. The fact that this normalization has historically not been done means that many vendors get away with delivering software that implements poorly—a fact that cannot be determined by simply reviewing a demonstration provided by a presales consultant. And it should go without saying that implementation success and implementation timelines are probabilistic. That is, TCO—as traditionally practiced—relies upon the assumption that all of the implementations will be successful and that the probability of success is equal between all applications. However, a TCO estimate without an approximation of the project's risk makes little sense. In fact, a failed implementation can have a "low TCO" if the buyer decides to cut their losses.

Strangely, companies do not estimate their probability of success prior to deciding which project to fund. Instead they take the naive assumption that all projects will succeed, even though IT projects have a high failure rate, even if the exact failure rate and the definition of failure is most often not specified.[31, 32] And this is not the end of the issue, because some live applications have been either significantly delayed or re-implemented. According to IDC, fifteen percent of survey respondents re-implemented their ERP software. However, in all the many TCO estimations that I have reviewed from other sources, I have yet to see a TCO that included the risk of either project failure or re-implementation. Entities that perform TCOs clearly have a strong tendency to assume perfect-world scenarios and with an assumption of **one hundred percent implementation success**. This faulty assumption reduces any interest to determine the differential risk between both the various applications that are part of the software selection, as well as the functionality employed by each of the applications.[33]

The Normalization Adjustments

The adjustments below were developed over time by simply comparing what facilitated cross-TCO comparisons:

1. Calculating the TCO Per Year

2. Adjusting for Differences Between SaaS and On-premises Solutions

3. Adjusting for Implementation Duration Differences

---

[31] The book *Enterprise Software Risk: Controlling the Main Risk Factors on IT Projects* covers this topic—a topic that, by the way, few entities that provide information on enterprise software have any interest in covering.

[32] I say "may," because the research is clear that companies often have no way of validating whether their project was a success because they have no formal measurements in place. The following quotation from research into the project success determination explains this fact—and a fact, which is frequently and easily glossed over when failure statistics are quoted, quite well. *"According to Parr and Shanks (2000) 'ERP project success simply means bringing the project in on time and on budget.' So, most ERP projects start with a basic management drive to target faster implementation and a more cost-effective project... Summarizing, the project may seem successful if the time/budget constraints have been met, but the system may still be an overall failure or vice versa. So these conventional measures of project success are only partial and possibly misleading measures when taken in isolation (Shenhar and Levy, 1997)"* — Measures of Success in Project Implementing Enterprise Resource Planning. Lazy journalists that write for the IT press have been quoting this "50%" number without checking the actual research on this topic.

[33] Different functionality has different likelihoods of success. Generally as functionality becomes more complex the success ratio declines—and applications have very different likelihoods of success, or implement-ability based upon factors such as the match between the business requirements and the application's functionality, how well the company is staffed in order to uptake the complex functionality, how well the more complex functionality is socialized during and after the implementation, etc.

4. Adjusting for Training Cost Differences

5. Adjusting for the Internal Support Costs Differences

6. Adjusting for Differences in the Number of Users

Calculating the TCO Per Year

A major issue in any TCO analysis is how long the application is used. If one TCO analysis assumes six years, while another assumes eight years, the software license and implementation costs are not amortized across the same number of years. Generally, the number of years should be kept consistent within a software category, but must be allowed to vary between software categories. For instance, ERP systems tend to have the longest implementation timelines of all enterprise software categories. In fact, ERP systems also tend to be the longest-lived enterprise applications with lifespans in companies averaging around ten years. It is also useful to break the TCO down to a per year value.

Adjusting for SaaS Versus On-premises Solutions

SaaS solutions have far fewer components to calculate than on-premises applications. In addition, the SaaS software vendor takes more of the risk on these costs, but because of their superior knowledge, they are in a much better position to do so. In this way, SaaS has a major advantage over on-premises solutions, and while this has been known for some time it has not been leveraged all that much by companies; as of the publication of this book, SaaS still only represents roughly **four** percent of all enterprise software revenues, something that was predicted to be much larger by this point. Something that SaaS vendors need in order to quickly increase the adoption of SaaS software is adherence to an ironclad privacy agreement so that they do not mine or sell the corporate information in the same way that is essentially part of the business model of Google and Facebook—but this is a large issue that requires an as yet unwritten book that combines a knowledge of law along with knowledge of SaaS/cloud delivered solutions.

To make the SaaS TCO estimation fit with the on-premises TCO estimations, it is necessary to add cost categories, which allows both TCO and on-premises solutions to be compared side by side, even though they do not have the same cost components. Simply comparing total costs for each delivery method is the most important issue. Effectively comparing on-premises solutions to SaaS solutions will be an important goal in the future as SaaS increases in popularity. In fact, our view is that a primary reason why SaaS is not more popular is that companies simply are not aware of the substantial cost benefits to SaaS-delivered solutions.

Adjusting for Implementation Duration

Different categories of software have different expected durations for implementation. For instance, SAP ERP, and big ERP in general has a very long and often painful implementation duration.[34] The duration of implementation of supply chain planning software can be long, particularly if complex methods are used. However, bill of material or recipe management applications are relatively quick to implement. Reporting applications can be implemented quickly if the application has a self service capability and orientation, or can be one of the longest implementations second only to ERP system. However, the determination of when the system is live must be when they are used to develop some substantial reports that meet business requirements, not when they are used to create some easy report. Amid all the discussions regarding "analytics" and "Big Data," some on-premises business intelligence applications take a **very long time** to deliver usable reports.

Furthermore, there are significant differences in how long it takes to implement various applications. Some applications are naturally easier to set up. Other applications are simply designed to enable the vendor to say they have certain functionality. Instead of relying upon good software design, vendors rely upon aggressive sales, paying off Gartner for a good rating and/or their partnerships with consulting companies to get their software sold. Therefore, any TCO evaluation means spending time with the application, either implementing the application or using the application in a real-world setting such as testing the introduction of new master data into the application and rating the difficulty, or asking the vendor to demonstrate specific functions, which can prove out the implement-ability and usability of the software.

---

[34] ERP consultants will often apply the *"no pain no gain"* euphemism to ERP projects, the logic being, *"Sure they are difficult, but they are worth it. Don't you want to be best in class?"* Research by SCM Focus clearly demonstrates that the pain is not worth the gain; many thousands of companies have gone through painful ERP implementations and there is no light waiting at the end of the tunnel. The primary beneficiaries were the ERP consultants and ERP consulting firms, not the implementing companies.

Adjusting for Training Costs

Different software categories have very different training costs because some enterprise software is simply easier to use than other software categories. Additionally, within the same software category, some software can be easier or more difficult to use. Training is typically estimated by multiplying the number of users who will receive training by the average training cost. However, this brings up the question of how many "courses" the users must take. On some projects, we have seen the frustration on the part of the company—often IT—that the users are not "getting" the system, and should be sent again to training. The short-term impact of training is greatly overestimated. Even after training, it takes considerable time until users reach their maximum efficiency with an application. Also, IT seems to treat all applications as equal in terms of usability, when in fact they are incredibly different. I have pointed this out in previous books, but I am in no way exaggerating when I say that at SCM Focus we can do a number of things with regard to forecasting using an inexpensive demand planning application that the largest multinationals **cannot do**, chiefly because we test a demand planning system that grades well in multiple aspects—and then we use those applications. We require very little training on this application; in fact, most of the training we have had has been on the software's advanced functions. Some of these specific items that so many companies have problems with in regard to forecasting software are explained in the SCM Focus Press book, *Supply Chain Forecasting Software.*

Bad software tends to require the most training. A good indicator of this is if users don't really use the software even through they have been sent to training. IT resources and decision makers will typically pin this on the fault of the users—with the remedy being that "they must be retrained." However, in most cases, IT is simply living in denial. It was part of the software selection process to include whether the users would be able to properly use the system. This should bring up the question as to whether users were even involved in the software selection decision—and in many cases they are not. A frequent mistake that companies make is not including the usability of the application into their software selection process. Instead the decision to purchase software is often made by executives who will never use the application. Software vendors with poor usability often do everything in their power to exclude users—knowing they will not be able to win them over. This is explained in the SCM Focus Press book, *Enterprise*

Software Selection: How to Pinpoint the Perfect Software Solution using Multiple Information Sources.

> *"Users need to be included in the audience during the demo, and their opinions should be solicited after the demo. Would they personally want to use the software? They should also be told to ask questions whenever they see fit and not at the end of the demo only. Users will pick up on things that executives will not. There is absolutely no logic to exclude the eventual users from a demo. When I worked at i2 Technologies, I recall that on one account the presales and sales team convinced the potential customers to keep users out of the demos. The sales and presales team explained to me that they knew the particular software they were showing was weak and that they would not be able to answer users' questions, so they needed to, in their words, "sell directly to the top.""*

In fact, too often the users are excluded from the demo, meaning that the demo tends to be a high-level affair. However, it is the **users** who ask the most pertinent questions related to how the software would be used in an everyday setting. Furthermore, the executives often do not even account for usability in their decision-making process, and then assume that users will quickly learn a system that is difficult to use.

> *"Companies reported that, following initial training, it took users anywhere from several **months to an entire year** before they were entirely comfortable using the application."* — Nucleus Research

Companies that exclude users from software selections should not be surprised when the users do not take to the application. Instead, the executive decision makers should say to themselves "of course." However, they don't; instead blaming the users or blaming Excel. At one client, a technique to force the users to use the ineffective solution that they had spent large sums of money on was to simply remove Excel from their users' computers.

In addition to the variability in training requirements between applications, some vendors have expensive training—expensive in terms of what the software vendor charges and in terms of the travel and time commitment. However, a few vendors (such as Demand Works) have come up with a creative way of reducing training costs by providing remote training that is partitioned out over time in smaller increments, a method that tends to enhance learning greatly and that is consistent with the continuous improvement principles that recognize that learning does not occur immediately and that users can only absorb so many new things in any interval. Much software training is very intensive and can leave the users overwhelmed. When they return to work the week following an intensive off-site training session, they find themselves further behind the work of their full-time job, and many of the things they learned will often quickly dissipate.

When calculating a training cost, it is important to factor not only the complexity of the software, but the design of the software, as well as the training model of the software vendor. For this reason, we have developed three different training multiples to be applied to the number of users of any implementation: Easy, Medium and Hard. Based upon this rating system, we assign a different training multiple to each application for which we create a TCO, and therefore a different cost.

Adjusting for the Internal Maintenance Costs

One of the most commonly underestimated areas of TCO is the internal maintenance costs. The same issues that apply to the training apply here. Software that is difficult to implement is also difficult to maintain and vice versa. Companies that breathe a sigh of relief after a difficult implementation probably shouldn't because the implementation difficulty is often—although not always—a good indicator of how much work will be required to maintain the application.

The relative ease of configuration, master data manipulation, and troubleshooting are all factors that we include in our estimates of how many people—and their percent allocation to the application and its integration and associated support—will be required for the life of the application in the implementing company.

How the application support is staffed changes depending upon the experience of the company. It can mean changing the makeup of the team, bringing on new resources, or retraining existing resources. However, that part of the planning is not a focus of the TCO. Instead, it's important to estimate the consumption of resources at the implementing company and whether they already exist. It will produce inaccurate TCO estimates to simply assume, as many companies do, that all applications within a software category will consume the same maintenance resources because this skews the estimates in favor of applications that are more expensive to maintain.

Adjusting for the Number of Users

Adjusting for the number of users is, of course, extremely significant for any TCO analysis, because the number of users is one of the most important drivers of cost. Applications scale in cost as the number of users increases. Therefore, a TCO that assumes 100 users will be higher with only 10 users—although the costs **will not scale in a linear fashion**. In fact, other things being held equal, the higher the number of users, the lower the user cost per user. This is a consistent relationship that holds true across all enterprise software categories. Unfortunately this insight often leads companies to attempt to use applications in more regions and in more divisions than it actually fits in order receive these "cost savings." That is direct cost savings of a lower cost application—without considering the cost savings or revenue enhancing capabilities of the functionality as matched to the business requirements. However, this is a standard IT focused blind spot that does not consider the functionality of the application. It is perplexingly simplistic, but is also extremely durable.

Many vendors price their software per user. If they do not, or if they have a multi-factor-pricing model, then the software cost per user can be estimated by taking several estimates at specific numbers of users and then triangulating back to the user estimate that is provided by the implementing company.

The cost per user is particularly useful for comparisons within a software category, as the estimated number of users for most applications within a software category will be the same. However, **the per user cost is not helpful** for making value comparisons **between** software categories, because different applications vary quite significantly based upon the type of application. For instance, the categories of software that are most broadly used are ERP systems and reporting/business intelligence systems, while the categories of software that are used most narrowly include specialty applications such as supply chain planning. In fact, the greater problem with a supply chain planning system is that too many people in the company use it and make changes; this is an issue because planning systems are supposed to be limited to a small number of users. Transaction processing systems such as ERP systems create changes (often to single records), and reporting/business intelligence systems simply allow users to view data rather than change data. However, supply chain planning systems allow users to change data and change aggregations of data, even though not too many people in the company should have this power. Therefore, the cost per user will be much higher for supply chain planning systems than for ERP systems. This is not a measurement of the value that these systems provide to the company, or whether a company should buy an application from one software category or another; it is simply the nature of these software categories and how they are designed to be used.

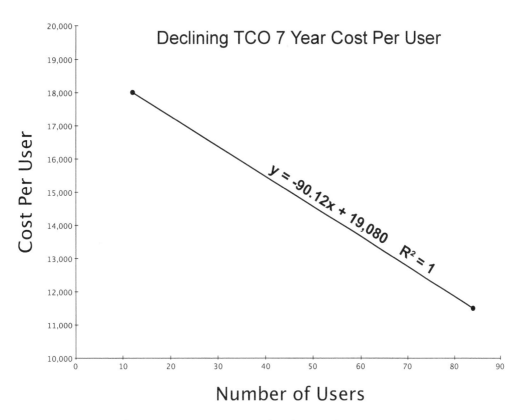

I added a regression formula, which is useful for making other estimates aside from the two data points that I have included above. For instance if a company had forty-two users, it could expect to pay $15,295 per user over a seven-year period, or $2,184 per user

per year. This is just one application; different applications have different relationships regarding how their costs per user decline as the number of users increases. Some articles have covered the cost per ERP user, but neglect to mention that the number of users for ERP systems tends to be high. Analysis that compares the cost per user per vendor without explaining the average number of users for each vendor will result in a misleading conclusion. Selectively releasing TCO statistics like this without showing the full context can easily result in the reader knowing less than before they learned the "statistic."

Using TCO for the Broadest Decision Making

This book is focused primarily on explaining the basics of TCO. However, what should be evident is that making multiple TCO calculations available leads to a variety of broader analyses. The problems with ERP are multifaceted, but two of the biggest issues are limited functionality combined with ERP's high TCO; added to these issues is how developing a dependency on ERP leads to the purchase of other applications with high TCO and low functionality. For some time the false argument of marijuana being a gateway drug was used to develop a highly punitive law enforcement system for marijuana smokers, including its classification as a Schedule 1 drug. However, a much stronger argument can be made that ERP is a "gateway drug" for companies to purchase other enterprise software with high TCO and low functionality than ever existed for marijuana being a gateway drug to harder drugs.

If a company builds a database of TCO calculations for its software selection projects, the company eventually ends up with a comprehensive TCO for categories of enterprise software. The graphic on the following page shows the broad ranging uses of TCO to support specific and broad decision-making.

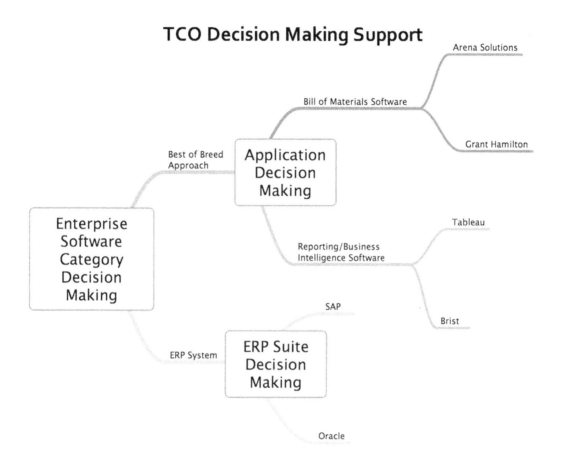

Conclusion

This chapter attempted to show some creative uses for TCO. One of the most interesting aspects of performing a TCO analysis between a wide number of applications is that not only are there great differences **between** the application categories (such as between reporting/business intelligence, supply chain planning, etc.), there are also great differences **within** application categories. Essentially, some applications with very high TCO are competing directly with applications with low TCO. Furthermore, there is not a strong relationship between an application's TCO and its quality, functionality or capability. What this means is that the enterprise software market is essentially inefficient. It also means that software selection is **incredibly** important because the variability in software value is so great.

CHAPTER 8

Conclusion

Total cost of ownership, or TCO, is the complete cost of owning something. TCO can be rearward looking—an accounting of what a purchase actually cost. However, in most cases a TCO analysis results in a forward projection or forecast. TCO for enterprise software is the overall sum of the costs of the four main TCO categories:

1. Software Cost

2. Hardware Cost

3. Implementation Cost

4. Maintenance Cost

TCO is discussed in the abstract as a "good thing" but is rarely calculated in reality. If you think back upon all of the purchases you made throughout your life, how many of them included the TCO on the price tag, along with the actual purchase price? There is a good reason (or good reasons) for this and they go by the names of sales and marketing. The last thing a company wants is for their prospective customers to know the total cost of an item. The one exception to this rule is if the vendor has a study that shows their product or service has a lower TCO than that of a competitor's product or service.

TCO is the base value for ROI: it is the "I" in ROI. A TCO must be calculated before an ROI can be calculated. ROI is the formalized analysis of the universal ratio between costs and benefits, which I referred to previously, and is focused on both the revenue and the costs of an investment. Determining the ROI of enterprise software is quite difficult because it means estimating the financial returns from software, which is a complex endeavor. Therefore, instead of producing ROI estimates, Software Decisions applies a rating system to the application, which is used in conjunction with the TCO estimate. This still allows the value of the software to be estimated, but without the necessity for an ROI calculation.

Correct TCO analysis requires effort; getting into the real detail of the costs and benefits of applications requires a combination of first-hand implementation experience as well as the analytical ability to perform the analysis. This analysis should be built from a level of detail such that the TCO flows naturally from the more thorough analysis.

While most software vendors hide their pricing information, all software vendors still like to discuss TCO in abstract terms as a "good thing."[35] Being in favor of TCO is like saying you are in favor of the American flag or apple pie; you're in favor of "goodness." You can't actually find anyone who opposes TCO in principle. But the devil is in the details. As long as nothing is quantified or the TCO studies are rigged, all vendors can say they have the lowest TCO. Most software vendors are not only against publishing TCO estimations, but are even against publishing

---

[35] The problem with hiding pricing information is that it is used as a control technique by software vendors in order to pry information from the buyers. It also greatly lengthens the process of finding out the pricing information and reduces the comparability of applications. In order to function efficiently, markets require published price information. There are some laws in the US on this topic for consumer products, but not for products purchased by corporations. On several occasions vendors have sent me non-disclosure agreements (NDA) that covered **pricing** information. However, this is a misuse of the NDA legal concept, as NDAs are designed to protect proprietary information—technical information, software intellectual property, and not pricing information. The legal phraseology implied that I could be sued for sharing pricing information with a third party if it damaged the company's business. However, wouldn't any sharing of pricing information, unless the software vendors were the low cost provider "damage their business?" Pricing information is part of what makes markets work and should be published.

pricing information for their applications on their websites. Software vendors cannot be relied upon to produce TCO estimates, and the best move is to disregard the software vendor's estimate. Secondly, no TCO study that is performed by a third party, but which is funded by a software vendor can be considered reliable. This should be obvious, but I have read the TCO estimates performed by third parties, which were funded in exactly this way, so someone is funding this work for a reason, and it is evidently convincing to someone.

Behind many poor decisions is a lack of proper TCO analysis, many consulting companies are also behind poor decisions. Consulting companies don't share the economic benefit of their clients' good decisions, and therefore are not incentivized to promote good decision-making on the part of their clients. If the consulting company is involved in the implementation (and almost all of them are), then having the consulting company performing the TCO violates the rule that was described in the beginning of this book, which is that any TCO analysis—or in fact any analysis—is that the entity performing the analysis must not have a vested interest in its outcome. Consulting companies are constantly putting out falsified information about the cost saving benefits of both ERP and outsourcing—which is not surprising as they are knee deep in selling these services. Software vendors and consulting companies are not the only entities that seek to suppress TCO estimations, but IT analysts and buying companies often have little interest in this information, as well.

Several entities disagree on whether or not a full TCO analysis should be a goal. In this section we will review the concerns leveled frequently at TCO. One of the entities—which could be labeled as anti-TCO and is influential in the area of enterprise software decision-making—is Forrester, the IT analyst firm.

In the field of enterprise software, one of the most amazing stories of the past several decades is the mass purchasing of ERP systems—purchases made without the customers searching for evidence that ERP systems are good investments. If they had looked, they would have found that the logic presented to sell ERP systems had no evidence to support it. Costs are often described in general parlance as the amount that we pay for things. However, economists look at costs quite a bit differently. Promoters of ERP tend to present any benefits of ERP without acknowledging that the time and effort spent on the ERP project could have gone into other initiatives. The comparison should be between the gains from those systems versus the gains from ERP systems.

Multiple estimations from software vendors cannot be simply accepted, but must be blended with experience in implementation. Many software vendors quote a 1:1 ratio between software costs and consulting costs. However, this is not the extent of implementation costs. Software vendors only consider their consulting costs (although sometimes they add in training) and do not include internal resource costs for the implementing company. Generally, consultants from the software vendor provide the best consulting value. As soon as an outside consulting company is involved, the costs of the implementation go up. Therefore, to account for all of this, Software Decisions uses higher multiples if a client states that they are using a major consulting company, and companies performing TCO analysis themselves should do the same.

Most vendors would not be happy with the implementation duration estimates developed by Software Decisions. However, these estimates are based upon years of analyzing how applications are actually implemented, which is far from the optimum values that are often quoted. We have performed the research, and the statistics are clearly on our side—enterprise software implementations take much longer than is generally assumed, not only by the software vendor, but also by the project management of the implementing company. If sixty percent of ERP implementations fail, and if the vast majority of ERP implementations miss their deadlines by significant durations, why are TCO estimates still based upon assumptions that do not include these very critical factors? Ninety-six percent of ERP implementations include moderate to extensive customizations. Customization results in high implementation costs, high continuous improvement costs, and high maintenance costs. Other software categories have various degrees of customization—almost always less than ERP—so ERP should receive the highest bump for coding-related implementation costs.

All TCO estimations are based upon some type of duration, that the company uses the application. While different software categories have different average usable durations, there is really no perfect way to estimate this value, and it is difficult to know how long the application will be in use in the company. Furthermore, an application that does not work very well can be kept too long—often for political reasons—while an application that is working well can be replaced due to issues that are related to what happens to be popular at the time.

Support resources include everyone required to support the application: technical, functional and management. It should never be assumed that the support "load" on internal resources **is equivalent, even between applications in the same software category**. There is a marked difference between vendors—and the degree to which the applications have been designed to be maintainable. This maintainability can be everything from how easy the application is to use (its usability: more usable applications require less hand-holding to accomplish tasks) to how straightforward it is to update its master data.

Developing the TCO estimations is the difficult part. The more interesting part is actually using the TCO, as there many varied uses. TCO can be used specifically or generally. For instance, once one has a handle on TCO for an application area, the TCO can be used to make future decisions after the purchase has been made. After TCO is developed, it can be put to use in supporting decision-making in a variety of ways. Companies should really have TCO analyses performed for all of their applications. It is quite common for companies to make decisions to extend use of their ERP system in some area, usually functionality that is known to be mediocre; however, the decision is driven by the desire to *"get more value from our ERP system"* or to *"leverage our ERP investment."* These can seem like desirable goals, until one begins to look through the lens of TCO. Overall, *"leveraging"* any current software, be it ERP or other software that the company owns, will not typically save the company more than fifteen percent of the TCO of the functionality in that area.

Strangely, companies do not estimate their probability of success prior to deciding which project to fund. Instead they take the naive assumption that all projects will succeed, even though IT projects have a high failure rate, even if the exact failure rate and the definition of failure is most often not specified.

To make the SaaS TCO estimation fit with the on-premises TCO estimations, it is necessary to add cost categories, which allows both TCO and on-premises solutions to be compared side by side, even though they do not have the same cost components. Simply comparing total costs for each delivery method is the most important issue. Effectively comparing on-premises solutions to SaaS solutions will be an important goal in the future as SaaS increases in popularity. In fact, our view is that a primary reason why SaaS is not more popular is that companies simply are not aware of the substantial cost benefits to SaaS-delivered solutions.

There are significant differences in how long it takes to implement various applications. Some applications are naturally easier to set up. Other applications are simply designed to enable the vendor to say they have certain functionality. Instead of relying upon good software design, vendors rely upon aggressive sales, paying off Gartner for a good rating and/or their partnerships with consulting companies to get their software sold. Therefore, any TCO evaluation means spending time with the application, either implementing the application or using the application in a real-world setting such as testing the introduction of new master data into the application and rating the difficulty, or asking the vendor to demonstrate specific functions, which can prove out the implement-ability and usability of the software.

One of the most commonly underestimated areas of TCO is the internal maintenance costs. The same issues that apply to the training apply here. Software that is difficult to implement is also difficult to maintain and vice versa. Companies that breathe a sigh of relief after a difficult implementation probably shouldn't because the implementation difficulty is often—although not always—a good indicator of how much work will be required to maintain the application.

Adjusting for the number of users is, of course, extremely significant for any TCO analysis, because the number of users is one of the most important drivers of cost. Applications scale in cost as the number of users increases. Therefore, a TCO that assumes 100 users will be higher with only 10 users—although the costs **will not scale in a linear fashion**. In fact, other things being held equal, the higher the number of users, the lower the user cost per user. However, **the per user cost is not helpful** for making value comparisons **between** software categories, because different applications vary quite significantly based upon the type of application. For instance, the categories of software that are most broadly used are ERP systems and reporting/business intelligence systems, while the categories of software that are used most narrowly include specialty applications such as supply chain planning.

This book has attempted to explain how to perform a proper TCO, as well as to explain the many uses of TCO. The TCO studies performed by Software Decisions have been able to enhance decision making through the use of TCO estimations performed across many software categories. This highlights a main theme of the book that while one TCO study can be useful—which is how TCO is primarily used—its usefulness increases greatly when TCO is performed for many applications and for many software categories. In fact, TCO for many software categories can be used to compare overall competing solution architectures, which is performed in the book *Replacing ERP: Breaking the ERP Habit with Flexible Applications at a Fraction of the Cost.* The most important conclusion from the research for this book is that companies do not do anywhere enough to leverage the power of TCO for their decision-making.

How to Use Independent Consultants for TCO

A company that is purchasing software may use this book or other sources to develop their own TCO. Generally, however, this is not a good idea. Purchasing companies do not have the experience with the application, and this experience is a critical component of performing the analysis.

Optimally an IT analyst firm would provide TCO analyses, as they have the broadest database of TCO data points. The problem is that the cost of TCO analysis or really any consulting from the major IT analyst firms is often exorbitant. As I stated in Chapter 3: "The State of Enterprise TCO," I am concerned that the consulting business that the IT analysts would receive from the vendors would pollute their TCO analyses. I am also concerned that IT analysts would not fully divulge the criteria that made up their TCO method, claiming that method as proprietary; instead, they would just share the results. This issue of not sharing the details of the research is documented in this book.

The sweet spot for IT analysts is not in doing detailed analysis, but in leveraging their very large network of clients in order to get to the bottom of TCO. However, because IT analysts do not actually work on projects, they have a higher-level perspective and they don't get the exposure to the reality of working on projects.

Continuing with concerns covered in Chapter 3: "The State of Enterprise TCO," consulting companies are too great a part of the software sales process to provide objective information about TCO or to provide any other input to software selection. I also discussed this fact in detail in my book, *Enterprise Software Selection*. If you contact a partner at a major consulting company who works out of the SAP practice, you will hear about the great benefits of SAP. If you contact a partner who works out of the Oracle practice—you get the idea.

So, if neither consulting companies nor IT analysts can be relied upon for dependable TCO analysis, then whom can a company turn to? I recommend independent consultants. One might observe that because I am an independent consultant myself, that my recommendation is an example of bias on my part. However, I was not always an independent consultant. One of the reasons I am an independent consultant is because I was repeatedly directed to do all the wrong things by major consulting companies that were intent on using me to distribute false information to their clients. I documented these experiences in an article, which I have included at the link below.

http://www.scmfocus.com/sapprojectmanagement/2011/03/my-education-in-corruption-by-the-major-consulting-firms/

I am extremely skeptical of information that comes from any of the major consulting companies—and many of the smaller ones. I saw how they undermine the analysis and twist it in order to meet a predetermined objective, even when they have a person like me who is known for analysis.

As an independent consultant, I am insulated from the corrupting influence of partners or other high-level individuals at consulting companies or at vendors that have steep sales quotas. I have written some of the most honest books about the state of enterprise software and implementation, and I have been able to do this because I am an independent consultant. Doing so has cost me projects, even as an independent consultant. However, providing honest information costs; it does not bring financial returns, which is why doing so is unpopular. Most of the money is in providing information that, while appearing to be honest, in fact is not, and in withholding critical and politically charged information.

The best-case scenario here is to find an independent consultant through something like LinkedIn. An independent consultant's experience in an application can be verified by the software vendor. However, a few rules should be followed to ensure that you control for bias as much as possible.

1. The independent consultant must have writing and analytical skills. There are many types of skills available on the independent market. The most common type of consultant is a pure configuration consultant. This type of consultant knows the switches to turn on and off in the application in which he or she specializes. The consultant tends to have moderately good communication skills (the communications skills are often limited by the necessity to also have the ability to grasp the complex configuration of an application), but do not generally perform TCO analysis. A good choice is a consultant with a mix of implementation experience and analytical experience.

2. The independent consultant should have many years of experience. This is important because when one is younger, it's more difficult to see consistencies between many implementations; younger consultants do not have broad experience on a large number of projects. Part of what you are hiring this consultant for is his or her personal database of projects of a similar type.

3. When the independent consultant is hired, it should be made clear that the consultant will only participate in the TCO phase. If the independent consultant believes that he or she may gain more work after the selection, this knowledge will bias the independent consultant most likely in favor of the software vendor—so that he or she can then work on the implementation. Single sourcing in any service area is truly a recipe for failure. Hiring more experts for smaller pieces of work is a more effective strategy, because it allows you to triangulate the information that is received from different entities. I do this myself when I hire attorneys or CPAs. There are various

levels of expertise, and no one knows everything. It's very easy to move outside of the service provider's area of expertise, where another expert is a better choice.

4. When searching for an independent consultant, it's important to find one with exposure to several applications in the area so that the consultant can compare and contrast for you the different applications. During software selection, multiple companies present to the prospect, and the independent consultant that you choose should be familiar with several of these applications.

5. During the interview with the independent consultant, determine if the consultant can see the positives and negatives of the applications that he or she will be helping you evaluate. If the consultant is simply a cheerleader for one application, then he or she will not be able to help you, even if quite knowledgeable in the technology.

6. Independent consultants move from project to project. TCO or ROI work, because they are shorter projects, are not as desirable to consultants as implementation projects, which are much longer contracts. You cannot expect an independent consultant to be available exactly when you want to review software vendors. However, you can hire independent consultants part time and remotely. That means they educate you remotely, listen in through a conference call, view the demo through a web conference, and review the material given to you remotely. This remote approach is quite a bit more cost effective and most independent consultants are amenable to this arrangement. On the other hand, if the independent consultant is available to work full time, there are advantages in that the consultant can provide a general education about the software category and can help with structuring the analysis for the software selection. In many cases, executive decision-makers are busy attending meetings or with other operational tasks, and employing someone who can really concentrate on the software selection can provide benefits.

Of course, the problem arises when no independent consultant can be found who has experience in the particular software that is part of the TCO. This is the case with smaller applications where the independent consulting market is simply not well developed. In this case, the best that can be done is to find an independent consultant with similar experience and exposure.

Other Books from SCM Focus

Bill of Materials in Excel, ERP, Planning and PLM/BMMS Software

http://www.scmfocus.com/scmfocuspress/the-software-approaches-for-improving-your-bill-of-materials-book/

Constrained Supply and Production Planning with SAP APO

http://www.scmfocus.com/scmfocuspress/select-a-book/constrained-supply-and-production-planning-in-sap-apo/

Enterprise Software Risk: Controlling the Main Risk Factors on IT Projects

http://www.scmfocus.com/scmfocuspress/it-decision-making-books/enterprise-software-project-risk-management/

Enterprise Software Selection: How to Pinpoint the Perfect Software Solution using Multiple Information Sources

http://www.scmfocus.com/scmfocuspress/it-decision-making-books/enterprise-software-selection/

Gartner and the Magic Quadrant: A Guide for Buyers, Vendors, Investors

http://www.scmfocus.com/scmfocuspress/it-decision-making-books/gartner-and-the-magic-quadrant/

Inventory Optimization and Multi-Echelon Planning Software

http://www.scmfocus.com/scmfocuspress/supply-books/the-inventory-optimization-and-multi-echelon-software-book/

Multi Method Supply Planning in SAP APO

http://www.scmfocus.com/scmfocuspress/select-a-book/multi-method-supply-planning-in-sap-apo/

Planning Horizons, Calendars and Timings in SAP APO

http://www.scmfocus.com/scmfocuspress/select-a-book/planning-horizons-calendars-and-timings-in-sap-apo/

Process Industry Manufacturing Software: ERP, Planning, Recipe, MES & Process Control

http://www.scmfocus.com/scmfocuspress/production-books/process-industry-planning/

Replacing Big ERP: Breaking the Big ERP Habit with Best of Breed Applications at a Fraction of the Cost

http://www.scmfocus.com/scmfocuspress/erp-books/replacing-erp/

Setting up the Supply Network in SAP APO

http://www.scmfocus.com/scmfocuspress/select-a-book/setting-up-the-supply-network-in-sap-apo/

SuperPlant: Creating a Nimble Manufacturing Enterprise with Adaptive Planning

http://www.scmfocus.com/scmfocuspress/production-books/the-superplant-concept/

Supply Chain Forecasting Software

http://www.scmfocus.com/scmfocuspress/the-statistical-and-consensus-supply-chain-forecasting-software-book/

Supply Planning with MRP, DRP and APS Software

http://www.scmfocus.com/scmfocuspress/supply-books/the-supply-planning-with-mrpdrp-and-aps-software-book/

The Real Story Behind ERP: Separating Fact from Fiction

http://www.scmfocus.com/scmfocuspress/erp-books/the-real-story-behind-erp/

Spreading the Word

SCM Focus Press is a small publisher. However, we pride ourselves on publishing the unvarnished truth, which most other publishers will not publish. If you felt like you learned something valuable from reading this book, please spread the word by adding a review to this book's page on Amazon.com.

Online Estimators

We offer a variety of estimators, at our companion site Software Decisions, one of which is a TCO estimator by various software categories. You can find out more about the TCO estimator at the Software Decisions website.

http://www.softwaredecisions.org

Links in the Book

Chapter 1

http://www.scmfocus.com/inventoryoptimizationmultiechelon/
2010/10/booz-allen-hamilton-misrepresents-inventory-
optimization-in-white-papers/

http://www.scmfocus.com/writing-rules/

http://www.scmfocus.com

http://www.scmfocus.com/scmfocuspress/it-decision-making-books/
enterprise-software-tco/

Chapter 3

http://www.scmfocus.com/sapprojectmanagement/2012/02/deloittes-
legal-intimidation-of-marin-county-and-what-can-be-learned-
from-it/

http://www.scmfocus.com/sapprojectmanagement/2012/02/has-
deloitte-bought-off-someone-inside-your-organization-as-they-did-
with-marin-county/

Chapter 4

http://www.scmfocus.com/supplyplanning/2011/07/09/what-is-your-supply-planning-optimizer-optimizing/

http://www.scmfocus.com/inventoryoptimizationmultiechelon/2011/05/how-costs-are-really-set-in-cost-optimization-implementations/

http://www.scmfocus.com/scmhistory/2010/07/how-analysts-got-everything-wrong-on-marketplaces/

http://www.scmfocus.com/demandplanning/category/demand-sensing/

Chapter 5

http://www.scmfocus.com/demandplanning/2010/07/outlier-removal/

Appendix A

http://www.scmfocus.com/sapprojectmanagement/2011/03/my-education-in-corruption-by-the-major-consulting-firms/

References

Angell, Marcia. *The Truth About the Drug Companies.* July 15, 2004.
http://www.wanttoknow.info/truthaboutdrugcompanies.

APQC. *Calculating the Total Cost of Ownership for Offshore Manufacturing* (2010).
http://www.operonresource.com/wp-content/themes/operon/assets/pdf/
Calc-total-cost-ownership-offshoring.pdf.

Baase, Sara. *IBM: Producer or Predator.* San Diego State University, 1974.
http://www-rohan.sdsu.edu/faculty/giftfire/ibm.html.

Bardach, Eugene. *A Practical Guide for Policy Analysis: The Eightfold Path to More Effective Problem Solving (4th Edition).* CQ Press: College Publishing Group, 2011.

Beheshti, Hooshang M. *What Managers Should Know About ERP/ERP II.* Management Research News, Vol. 29, No. 4, pp. 184–193, 2006.

Biello, David. *Grass Makes Better Ethanol than Corn Does.* Scientific American. January 8, 2008.
http://www.scientificamerican.com/article.cfm?id=grass-makes-better-ethanol-than-corn.

Bridgewater, Adrian. *ERP is Dead, Long Live Two-Tier ERP.* December 12, 2012.
http://www.computerweekly.com/blogs/cwdn/2012/12/erp-is-dead-long-live-two-tier-erp.html.

Chiappinelli, Chris. *New ERP Paradigm Challenges Old Assumptions.* March 2, 2011. http://www.techmatchpro.com/article/2011/3/new-erp-paradigm-challenges-old-assumptions.

Clarke, Gavin. *Larry 'Shared Databases are Crap' Ellison Reveals Shared Oracle Database.* October 1, 2012. http://www.theregister.co.uk/2012/10/01/ellison_oow_2012_database_cloud/.

Columbus, Louis. *ERP Prediction for 2013: The Customer Takes Control.* Forbes. January 07, 2013. http://www.forbes.com/sites/louiscolumbus/2013/01/07/erp-prediction-for-2013-the-customer-takes-control/.

Corn Ethanol. Accessed July 3, 2013. http://en.wikipedia.org/wiki/Corn_ethanol.

Credit Rating Agency. Accessed August 11, 2013. http://en.wikipedia.org/wiki/Credit_rating_agency.

Cullinan, Charles, Sutton, Steven G., and Arnold, Vicky. *Technology Monoculture: ERP Systems, "Technology Process Diversity" and the Threat to the Information Technology Ecosystem.* Advances in Accounting Behavioral Research, Volume 13 13–30, 2010.

Elragal, Ahmed and Al-Serafi, Ayman. *The Effect of ERP System Implementation on Business Performance: An Exploratory Case-Study.* http://www.ibimapublishing.com/journals/CIBIMA/2011/670212/670212.pdf.

Eller, Claudia. *Warner Bros. to outsource jobs overseas.* LA Times. January 10, 2009. http://articles.latimes.com/2009/jan/10/business/fi-warner10.

Enterprise Resource Planning. Accessed March 15, 2013. http://en.wikipedia.org/wiki/Enterprise_resource_planning.

ERP Budget & Cost Considerations: Moving from QuickBooks to ERP. http://blog.e2benterprise.com/erp-budget-cost-considerations-moving-from-quickbooks-to-erp-part-5-of-8-part-series/.

Eskilsson, Helene, Nystrom, Christiana, and Windler, Maria. *ERP System and Effects: A Comparison of Theory and Practice.* Gotenborg University, 2003.

Fauscette, Michael. *Maintaining ERP Systems: The Cost of Change.* IDC, May 2013.

Ferreira, John and Prokopets, Len. *Does Offshoring Still Make Sense?* January, 2009. http://www.areadevelopment.com/article_pdf/id44472_does-offshoring-still-make-sense.pdf.

Finke, Nikki. *Warner Bros Announces 800 Layoffs.* January 20, 2009.
    http://www.deadline.com/2009/01/as-expected-warner-bros-announces-layoffs/.

Free Speech or Knowing Misrepresentation? February 5, 2013.
    http://www.economist.com/blogs/schumpeter/2013/02/rating-agencies.

Gartner. *IT Spending: How Do Your Stack Up?* Gartner, 2003.

Greenbaum, Joshua. *Rethinking TCO: Towards a More Viable and Useful Measure of
    IT Costs.* Enterprise Application Consulting, Spring 2005.

Hiltonsmith, Robert. *The Retirement Savings Drain: The Hidden and Excessive Costs
    of 401(k)s.* Demos. (2012)

History of IBM. Accessed July 26, 2013.
    http://en.wikipedia.org/wiki/History_of_IBM#1969:_Antitrust.2C_the_
    Unbundling_of_software_and_services.

Hopper, Grace. *The Decline of Single Instance Big ERP. Why Two-Tier ERP is on the
    CIO Agenda.* April 11, 2011.
    http://www.netsuiteblogs.com/blog/2011/03/the-decline-of-single-insta nce-big-erp-
    why-two-tier-erp-is-on-the-cio-agenda.html.

Jacobs, F Robert and Weston Jr, FC. *ERP – A Short History.* Journal of Operations
    Management. (2007).

Kanaracus, Chris. *Air Force Scraps Massive ERP Project After Racking up $1 Billion
    in Costs.* November 14, 2012.
    http://www.cio.com/article/721628/Air_Force_scraps_massive_ERP_project_after_
    racking_up_ 1_billion_in_costs.

Kimberling, Eric. *Are Two-Tier ERP Systems Finally Becoming Mainstream?*
    December 19, 2012.
    http://panorama-consulting.com/are-two-tier-erp-systems-finally-becoming-
    mainstream/.

Kimberling, Eric. *Top Ten Predictions for the Global ERP Industry in 2013.* November
    20, 2012.
    http://panorama-consulting.com/top-ten-predictions-for-the-global-erp-industry-
    in-2013/.

Klahr, Sue. *Oracle Imposes Oppressive Maintenance Costs on Sun Hardware Clients.*
    December 5, 2011.
    http://smarterquestions.org/2011/12/oracle-imposes-oppressive-maintenance-
    costs-on-sun-hardware-clients/.

Koch, Christopher, Slater, Derek, and Baatz, E. *The ABCs of ERP.* http://paginas.fe.up.pt/~mgi00011/ERP/abcs_of_erp.htm.

Jurtras, Cindy. *The High Cost of Business Disruption in Modifying and Maintaining ERP,* Mint Jutras. (2013)

MacCormack, Alan. *Evaluating Total Cost of Ownership for Software Platforms: Comparing Apples, Oranges and Cucumbers.* AEI-Brookings Joint Center for Regulatory Studies, 2013.

Major, Christine. *Demandware Announces Research that Reveals TCO Analysis of eCommerce Solutions Often Fail to Expose True Costs.* November 20, 2012. http://finance.yahoo.com/news/demandware-announces-research-reveals-tco-143000739.html.

Mallory, James. *ERP Budget & Cost Considerations: Moving from QuickBooks to ERP.* April 24, 2013. http://blog.e2benterprise.com/erp-budget-cost-considerations-moving-from-quickbooks-to-erp-part-5-of-8-part-series/.

Mann, Charles. *Why Software Is So Bad.* MIT Technology Review Magazine. July 1, 2002. http://www.technologyreview.com/featuredstory/401594/why-software-is-so-bad/.

Manufacturing. Accessed July 12, 2013. https://en.wikipedia.org/wiki/Manufacturing.

Moon, Andy. *Are the Rewards of ERP Systems Worth the Risk?* March 27, 2008. http://www.techrepublic.com/blog/tech-news/are-the-rewards-of-erp-systems-worth-the-risk/2133.

Netsuite. *What Is ERP?* August 27, 2013. http://www.netsuite.com/portal/resource/articles/erp/what-is-erp.shtml.

Opportunity Cost. Accessed June 22, 2013. https://en.wikipedia.org/wiki/Opportunity_cost.

Oracle Imposes Oppressive Maintenance Costs on Sun Hardware. December 5, 2011. http://smarterquestions.org/2011/12/oracle-imposes-oppressive-maintenance-costs-on-sun-hardware-clients/.

Overby, Stephanie. *IT Increases Application Outsourcing Despite Disappointing Strategic Value.* July 12, 2013. http://www.cio.com/article/736275/IT_Increases_Application_Outsourcing_Despite_Disappointing_Strategic_Value.

Overby, Stephanie. *The Hidden Costs of Offshore Outsourcing.* September 1, 2003. http://www.cio.com/article/29654/The_Hidden_Costs_of_Offshore_Outsourcing.

Pabo-Nazao, Placid and Raymond, Louis. *In House Development as an Alternative for ERP Adoption by SMES: A Critical Case Study.* 17th European Conference on Information Systems, 2009.

Philips, Steven Scott. *Control Your ERP Destiny: Reduce Project Costs, Mitigate Risks, and Design Better Business Solutions.* Street Smart ERP Publications, 2012.

PlanetTogether. *APS Product Training.*

Prouty, Kevin and Castellina, Nick. *To ERP or Not to ERP.* April, 2011. http://www.plex.com/wordpress/wp-content/uploads/2012/05/Aberdeen-ERPvsNoERP.pdf.

Proving a Negative. Accessed March 15, 2013. http://en.wikipedia.org/wiki/Proving_a_negative.

Rathmann, Charles. *Cloud ERP Software Preferences Study.* IFS, 2013.

Reichman, Andrew and Staten, James. *TCO is Overrated.* August 26, 2008. http://www.forrester.com/TCO+Is+Overrated/fulltext/-/E-RES44545?docid=44545.

Rettig, Cynthia. *The Trouble With Enterprise Software.* MIT Sloan (Fall 2007). http://sloanreview.mit.edu/article/the-trouble-with-enterprise-software/.

Rich, Michael. *Perpetuating RAND's Tradition of High-Quality Research.* November, 2011.
http://www.rand.org/standards.html.

Rohm, Ted. *To ERP or Not to ERP, That is the C-Level Question.* February 22, 2013. http://blog.technologyevaluation.com/blog/2013/02/22/to-erp-or-not-to-erp-that-is-the-c-level-question/.

Ruffinatti, Adrián. *Costo Total de Propiedad Estrategias en la Industria del Software.* Amazon Digital Services, 2010.

Savitz, Eric. *The End of ERP.* Forbes Magazine. February 09, 2012. http://www.forbes.com/sites/ciocentral/2012/02/09/the-end-of-erp/2/.

Schmidt, Marty. *Total Cost of Ownership.* Last modified October 25, 2013. http://www.business-case-analysis.com/total-cost-of-ownership.html.

Shahin, Dezdar. Sulaiman, Ainin. *Measures of Success in Project Implementing Enterprise Resource Planning.* International Journal of Business Performance Management, January 1, 2011.

Single Instance ERPs are Scarce, says Study. March, 2006.
http://www.cimaglobal.com/Thought-leadership/Newsletters/Insight-e-magazine/
Insight-March-2006/Single-instance-ERPs-are-scarce-says-study/.

Snapp, Shaun. *Constrained Supply and Production Planning with SAP APO.* SCM
Focus Press, 2013.

Snapp, Shaun. *Enterprise Software Risk: Controlling the Main Risk Factors on IT
Projects.* SCM Focus Press, 2014.

Snapp, Shaun. *Enterprise Software Selection: How to Pinpoint the Perfect Software
Solution Using Multiple Information Sources.* SCM Focus Press, 2013.

Snapp, Shaun. *Gartner and the Magic Quadrant. A Guide for Buyers, Vendors and
Investors.* SCM Focus Press, 2013.

Snapp, Shaun. *Planning Horizons, Calendars and Timings in SAP APO.* SCM Focus
Press, 2013.

Snapp, Shaun. *Process Industry Manufacturing Software: ERP, Planning, Recipe,
MES & Process Control.* SCM Focus Press, 2013.

Snapp, Shaun. *Replacing Big ERP: Breaking the Big ERP Habit with Best-of-Breed
Applications at a Fraction of the Cost.* SCM Focus Press, 2013.

Snapp, Shaun. *SuperPlant: Creating a Nimble Manufacturing Enterprise with
Adaptive Planning Software.* SCM Focus Press, 2013.

Snapp, Shaun. *Supply Chain Forecasting with Software.* SCM Focus Press, 2012.

Snapp, Shaun. *Supply Planning with MRP, DRP and APS Software.* SCM Focus
Press, 2012.

Snapp, Shaun. *The Bill of Materials in Excel, ERP, Planning and PLM/BMMS
Software.* SCM Focus Press, 2013.

Snapp, Shaun. *The Real Story Behind Two-tiered ERP.* SCM Focus Press, 2014.

Sommer, Brian. *ERP's Franken-soft and How Workday Avoids it.* November 13, 2012.
http://www.zdnet.com/erps-franken-soft-and-how-workday-avoids-it-7000007200/.

Stanley, George. *4 ERP Tips for FIAR Compliance.* IFS, 2013.

Strengths and Weaknesses of Total Cost of Ownership. Nucleus Research, 2007.
http://nucleusresearchblog.com/2013/06/18/the-argument-against-tco/.

Tableau Online Total Cost of Ownership Calculator.
http://www.freakalytics.com/2013/07/21/tableau-online-tco-calculator/.

Tautology. Last modified October 4, 2013.
http://en.wikipedia.org/wiki/Tautology.

Technology Evaluation Centers. *The Best of Class Financial System Strategy: An Alternative to ERP Platforms.* (2010)

The Real ROI from i2 Supply Chain Management. Nucleus Research, 2003.

Themistocleous, Marinos, Irani, Zahir and O'Keefe, Robert. *M ERP and Application Integration: Exploratory Survey.* Business Process Management Journal, Vol. 7 Iss. 3, pp.195–204.

Wagner, David. *Old & Bad ERP All Over Manufacturing.* April 17, 2013.
http://www.enterpriseefficiency.com/author.asp?section_id=1151&doc_id=262241.

Wainewright, Phil. *ERP, RIP? Cloud financials and revenue management in 2013.* January 4, 2013.
http://www.zdnet.com/erp-rip-cloud-financials-and-revenue-management-in-2013-7000009376/.

Wailgum, Thomas. *ERP Sticker Shock: Maintenance, Upgrades and Customizations.* September 23, 2010.
http://www.cio.com/article/618117/ERP_Sticker_Shock_Maintenance_Upgrades_and_Customizations.

Wailgum, Thomas. *SaaS ERP Has Buzz, But Who Are the Real Players?* March 10, 2010.
http://www.cio.com/article/572463/SaaS_ERP_Has_Buzz_But_Who_Are_the_Real_Players.

Wailgum, Thomas. *Want to Save $10 Million or More on ERP? Don't Buy Oracle or SAP.* February 26, 2009.
http://blogs.cio.com/thomas_wailgum/want_to_save_10_million_or_more_on_erp_dont_buy_oracle_or_sap?source=nlt_cioenterprise.

Wailgum, Thomas. *Why ERP Is Still So Hard.* September 09, 2009.
http://www.cio.com/article/501656/Why_ERP_Is_Still_So_Hard.

Weisenthal, Joe. *Here's the Trend Obama Is Fighting, If He Wants to Save American Manufacturing.* August 23, 2010.
http://www.businessinsider.com/chart-of-the-day-manufacturing-employment-as-a-percentage-of-total-non-farm-payrolls-2010-8.

What That Car Really Costs to Own: Knowing a Vehicle's Cost Over Time Can Save You Thousands in the Long Haul. August, 2012.
http://www.consumerreports.org/cro/2012/12/what-that-car-really-costs-to-own/index.htm.

Wolpe, Toby. *When SAP Sprawl is Cool: Could Cutting Back Your ERP be More Pain Than it's Worth?* May 9, 2013. http://www.zdnet.com/are-businesses-wasting-millions-on-sap-erp-they-dont-need-7000015133/.

Worthen, Ben. *Extreme ERP Makeover.* December 9, 2003. http://www.cio.com.au/article/181834/extreme_erp_makeover/?pp=5.

Author Profile

Shaun Snapp is the Founder and Editor of SCM Focus. SCM Focus is one of the largest independent supply chain software analysis and educational sites on the Internet.

After working at several of the largest consulting companies and at i2 Technologies, he became an independent consultant and later started SCM Focus. He maintains a strong interest in comparative software design, and works both in SAP APO, as well as with a variety of best-of-breed supply chain planning vendors. His ongoing relationships with these vendors keep him on the cutting edge of emerging technology.

Primary Sources of Information and Writing Topics

Shaun writes about topics with which he has first-hand experience. These topics range from recovering problematic implementations, to system configuration, to socializing complex software and supply chain concepts in the areas of demand planning, supply planning and production planning.

More broadly, he writes on topics supportive of these applications, which include master data parameter management, integration, analytics, simulation and bill of material management systems. He covers management aspects of enterprise software ranging from software policy to handling consulting partners on SAP projects.

Shaun writes from an implementer's perspective and as a result he focuses on how software is actually used in practice rather than its hypothetical or "pure release note capabilities." Unlike many authors in enterprise software who keep their distance from discussing the realities of software implementation, he writes both on the problems as well as the successes of his software use. This gives him a distinctive voice in the field.

Secondary Sources of Information
In addition to project experience, Shaun's interest in academic literature is a secondary source of information for his books and articles. Intrigued with the historical perspective of supply chain software, much of his writing is influenced by his readings and research into how different categories of supply chain software developed, evolved, and finally became broadly used over time.

Covering the Latest Software Developments
Shaun is focused on supply chain software selections and implementation improvement through writing and consulting, and bringing companies some of the newest technologies and methods. Some of the software developments that Shaun showcases at SCM Focus and in books at SCM Focus Press have yet to reach widespread adoption.

Education
Shaun has an undergraduate degree in business from the University of Hawaii, a Masters of Science in Maritime Management from the Maine Maritime Academy and a Masters of Science in Business Logistics from Penn State University. He has taught both logistics and SAP software.

Software Certifications

Shaun has been trained and/or certified in products from i2 Technologies, Servigistics, ToolsGroup and SAP (SD, DP, SNP, SPP, EWM).

Contact

Shaun can be contacted at: shaunsnapp@scmfocus.com.

Abbreviations

CIO: Chief Information Officer

CPU: Central Processing Unit

DOD: Department of Defense

ERP: Enterprise Resources Planning

GAAP: Generally Accepted Accounting Principles

NPV: Net Present Value

RAND: Research and Development

RCO: Relative Cost of Operation

ROI: Return on Investment

SaaS: Software as a Solution

TCO: Total Cost of Ownership

USAF: United States Air Force

Y2K: Year 2000

www.ingramcontent.com/pod-product-compliance
Lightning Source LLC
LaVergne TN
LVHW080059070326
832902LV00014B/2318